Quality Assurance
and Evaluation
in the Lifelong Learning Sector

Quality Assurance and Evaluation
in the Lifelong Learning Sector

Jane Wood and John Dickinson

First published in 2011 by Learning Matters Ltd

British Library Cataloguing in Publication Data
A CIP record for this book is available from the British Library.

ISBN: 978 1 84445 836 3

This book is also available in the following ebook formats:
Adobe ebook ISBN: 9781844458387
EPUB ebook ISBN: 9781844458370
Kindle ISBN: 9780857250445

Cover design by Topics
Text design by Code 5
Project management by Deer Park Productions, Tavistock
Typeset by PDQ Typesetting Ltd, Newcastle under Lyme
Printed and bound in Great Britain by Bell & Bain Ltd, Glasgow

Learning Matters Ltd
20 Cathedral Yard
Exeter EX1 1HB
Tel: 01392 215560
info@learningmatters.co.uk
www.learningmatters.co.uk

Mixed Sources
Product group from well-managed forests and other controlled sources
www.fsc.org   Cert no. TT-COC-002769
© 1996 Forest Stewardship Council
FSC

Contents

The authors   vii

Acknowledgements   vii

Introduction   ix

1 Concepts of quality   1

2 Delivering quality in the classroom   14

3 External inspection   28

4 Internal inspection   39

5 Assessment: moderation and verification   49

6 Listening to learners and evaluating learners' experience   61

7 Culture, ethos and values   75

8 Professionalism and accountability   90

9 Working in teams   104

10 Putting it all together   115

Index   127

The authors

Jane Wood is Assistant Head of Undergraduate Professional Development and senior lecturer in Post-Compulsory Education and Training at Edge Hill University. She has been a Quality Manager in a college and has over 20 years' experience teaching in the sector.

John Dickinson began his career as a residential social worker. In 1982 he joined Kirkby College of Further Education on Merseyside. He taught child care, health and social care and A Level and GCSE Psychology. He has been working in teacher training for FE staff since 1990. He is currently a Senior Lecturer at Edge Hill and an original member of the Post-Compulsory Education and Training team.

Dedication

Jane would like to dedicate this book to Alexander James Hughes, my beautiful baby grandson.

John would like to dedicate this book to Jane, Andrew and Philip, with thanks for their support.

Acknowledgements

We would like to thank David Ryan for all his help and support.

We would also like to thank the following colleagues for their contributions: Jane Dickinson; Chris Horne; Jane Martin; Lorraine Roberts; George Woodall.

Introduction

After seven years at my college, I applied for the job of cross-college curriculum quality manager. Having been a curriculum manager it seemed reasonable to assume, naively, that I understood the role of the quality department!

Once in post, I realised that the quality department was myself and my boss for a college with thousands of students and hundreds of staff. How, then, to do this job for the whole college?

What soon became apparent is that quality is the job of everyone in the college and not just the quality department. If we want to give our students the best experience then everyone has to buy into the quality agenda and do their jobs to the highest standards possible.

Quality is the elephant in the room, this thing that most people try to ignore or to pass off as someone else's job when actually it is everyone's responsibility.

In delivering a module about quality to our trainee teachers we realised that there are no up-to-date textbooks to support the module. No books exist that discuss this 'elephant in the room' in terms that new teachers or teachers new to management can use to understand the reasons behind the decisions of government and management and the reality of the audit culture in the sector.

This book is based squarely on our own experiences in the sector together with our own research. It has its foundation in the real-life practical situations that occur in the sector.

We envisage the book as a simple source of reference and a guide to assist trainee or new teachers, whether they are in service or pre-service, to undertake the full role of the teacher with confidence and pride.

The chapters aim to provide a journey through the world of quality and evaluation and to include real-life case studies.

It has been a collaboration between colleagues and has been influenced every step of the way by the experiences of the many trainee teachers we teach, observe, tutor and support in our jobs as senior lecturers at Edge Hill University.

We are only ever as good as the students we teach, their success is our success and their failure is our responsibility.

All we can say now is good luck, enjoy the book and look out for that elephant!

Jane Wood and John Dickinson, 2011

1
Concepts of quality

This chapter is designed to:

- offer you an introduction to the concepts of quality assurance and quality improvement;
- outline the key indicators of quality that have been established in the lifelong learning sector;
- explore how staff in the sector have been expected to engage with various quality initiatives;
- signpost some of the policies and procedures with which you will be involved as you move towards Qualified Teacher Learning and Skills status.

It addresses the following Professional Standards for QTLS:

AS 4 Reflection and evaluation of their own practice and their continuing professional development as teachers.

AK 4.3 Ways to reflect, evaluate and use research to develop own practice, and to share good practice with others.

AS 7 Improving the quality of their practice.

AK 7.1 Organisational systems and processes for recording learner information.

AK 7.2 Own role in the quality cycle.

AS 7.3 Ways to implement improvements based on feedback received.

Introduction

In God we trust. Everyone else brings data.

The above quote, attributed to Dr W Edwards Deming, considered to be one of the 'quality gurus', provides an introduction to the focus and purpose of this book. It signposts the fact that quality is about information, in this quote information that is called data. Now data make take many forms: it may be numerical; it may be illustrated in charts and graphs; it may be the summation of opinion captured through surveys. However, whatever form it takes, Deming's words direct us to the fact that to be involved with quality we are going to be involved in measuring something, judging what we have measured and in responding to the outcomes of that measurement.

It is to be hoped that the mention of data does not immediately put you off, because you will find that it is a requirement of employment in the sector today that you, as a practising teacher, trainer or tutor, are able to use data in its broadest sense. You will need to identify the key elements of your work; to be able to measure the effectiveness of your work against a number of criteria; to evaluate your effectiveness in terms of teaching and learning and to evaluate your students' overall experience. Furthermore, armed with this information you will use it to successfully improve for next time. This, in other words, is to be involved in the processes of quality assurance and evaluation and consequently to improve the quality of your work.

We believe it is important to signpost and emphasise just how much the approaches to quality currently in use within the sector lay an expectation of engagement on every member of the organisation. While it may not have been uncommon in the past to hear colleagues say something like, 'but I came into FE to teach, not to do customer surveys', the inescapable fact is that stakeholders such as your employer, the Department for Education, Ofsted, the Institute for Learning (IfL) and Lifelong Learning UK (LLUK) all want to see every teacher and trainer in the sector involved in the processes of quality assurance and evaluation and of being capable of creating quality improvement. We would also add that it is our belief that the best teachers have always done this – indeed, why would you want to do anything else but be the best you can be?

Drawing on an overview of the development of quality assurance in further education (FE) over the last 25 years it is the intention of this book to explore and establish an approach to quality assurance and evaluation that is both supportive and effective. We hope to equip you with knowledge and skills so that, as a fully engaged professional, you are informed and proactive about how to provide the best quality of teaching and learning experience to your students. We intend also to encourage you to recognise that, at times, quality systems within human organisations can sometimes be badly designed, badly managed or ineffectively implemented and that you will have to work within such restrictions and nevertheless sustain the quality of what you do. Thus, there is a theme of critical consideration within this book, scrutinising the development of quality assurance, the use of evaluation and perceptions of quality improvement within the sector and their immediate impact on practitioners and learners alike.

The goal is to provide you with a confident knowledge base and useful understanding of processes and practice and also to encourage a degree of criticality to be applied wherever you find yourself working. While the application of quality assurance and quality improvement policies and processes within the sector has brought tangible benefits in the main, there remain aspects that are arguably ineffective or sometimes even damaging within the quality 'culture' and therefore it is necessary to ensure a balanced and informed approach.

What do we mean by quality?

REFLECTIVE TASK

Consider the following questions and note down your answers.
- What is your definition of quality?
- Do you associate it with people, products, or both?
- Does it differ depending on your experience or your expectations?

You may have found it easy to define quality; you may feel it is common sense – about doing your best or producing the best, meeting a standard or working well – or you may have recognised that, 'it all depends on ...'.

Indeed, it depends on many things and a brief visit to the many popular educational columns and blogs available in the press or via the web will provide polarised views on how strongly people feel about the 'quality' of education today. Is it really all about the 'dumbing down' of education and falling standards? Is it about school leavers who are unemployable because they can't read and write or do simple maths? Is it that exams are easier these days? Or is there evidence of the radical innovation of learning that is transforming young people's development, generating new knowledge and new skills in emerging technology and new fields of opportunity?

Since that debate is highly politicised and significantly shaped by the social and educational background of the contributors, it is not the intention of this book to try to answer those questions or engage specifically in those arguments. Rather, while the debate runs on, we wish to ensure that you are able to engage with, and benefit from, a positive approach to quality, informed by your own definition and your own context, but also responsive to existing policy and practice in the sector.

PRACTICAL TASK PRACTICAL TASK **PRACTICAL TASK** PRACTICAL TASK **PRACTICAL TASK**

Complete the following tasks.
- Make a note of three characteristics of 'good' teaching.
- Then rate yourself on each characteristic.

So, by your characteristics and scoring system are you a good teacher? Would your students, colleagues, or mentor agree?

- Now add two more characteristics to your list of 'good' teaching and rate yourself on those also.

Some questions to consider for reflection.

- Is there a noticeable difference in the type of criteria you employed when first asked to characterise 'good' teaching and those you chose when asked to extend your list?
- How did you rate yourself? Did you use a concept of high/low or maybe you gave yourself a score? (Perhaps you didn't do the task because 'it's impossible to measure what you mean by "good"'.)
- Did you consider if there would be a difference between how others rate you and how you rated yourself?
- Did you think there should be different systems for rating yourself and being rated by others?

If you found the task a little difficult or hard to pin down, don't worry. If we look at the origins and development of the whole approach to 'quality' you will see why this might be the case.

Recognising the key concepts

As we will frequently be using the terms 'quality assurance', 'evaluation' and 'quality improvement' it will be helpful to establish their meaning now. A point to note is that the models of quality management we are using within post-compulsory education in the UK have come from international (mostly American and Japanese) models of quality management. It is necessary to recognise this as a starting point, but also to be comfortable with some generally shared, non-expert definitions as well. This, after all, is an introductory text for aspiring teachers in the UK post-compulsory sector, not a text for aspiring MBA candidates.

Quality assurance

The International Organization for Standardization (ISO) defines quality assurance (QA) as *a set of activities intended to establish confidence that quality requirements will be met* (Praxiom, 2010).

(Based on the original British Standards Institute BS5750 Standard for Quality Assurance, ISO 9000 is a 'family' of standards for quality management systems and is a leading benchmark that organisations strive for to confirm their management credibility.)

In the context of post-compulsory education we can take this definition to mean the identification of those aspects of our work that can be seen to be the core activities, such as recruitment, induction, teaching and learning, support and assessment, by which the quality of the overall learner experience can be determined. The intention of an education provider to achieve effective quality assurance is an attempt to guarantee the quality of provision and to instil confidence in the learner.

In simple terms, if quality assurance is established it should ensure the best learning outcomes for each individual because every aspect of provision will be planned and delivered as well as it can be.

Evaluation

Within education the term 'evaluation' is sometimes used interchangeably with assessment (not surprisingly since the *Oxford Dictionary* gives one definition of evaluation to be 'assessment'). However, we would encourage you to recognise the two as distinct and separate.

Assessment is the process of measuring a learner's performance within a formal or informal task designed to evidence what has been learned and to what level.

Evaluation is the considered judgement about the quality of a product, a process, an experience.

The approach we will adopt is that you, as a teacher or trainer, assess your learners and provide the outcomes of those assessments to relevant parties such as the learners themselves, your colleagues and the relevant award bodies.

The learners will evaluate the quality of your teaching and they may also be invited to evaluate other aspects of the organisation's provision. You will also be involved in evaluation through response to this feedback from learners and through your own personal reflection.

Evaluation will also be undertaken by internal and external stakeholders because it has been established as common practice as the way to sustain quality assurance and, where necessary, to drive quality improvement.

Quality improvement

According to the ISO the definition of quality improvement (QI) is *part of quality management focused on increasing the ability to fulfil quality requirements* (Praxiom, 2010).

In other words, quality improvement refers to anything that enhances your organisation's ability to meet its quality requirements. The requirements for quality in a post-compulsory setting are those core activities identified above and the foremost person involved in all of those will be you.

Quality improvement will be achieved by first of all being recognised as needed and then by implementing an effective strategy that will address any deficiencies in whichever area of provision. Your most immediate responsibility will be for the quality of teaching and learning and here you can make immediate use of the evaluation described previously. You will evaluate your learners' achievements, year on year, cohort by cohort, to make an informed decision about the quality of your work. You will have feedback from your learners in the form of evaluations that will provide a focus for your personal and professional reflection, as well as possible areas to discuss with a line manager at appraisal.

These three key concepts will be evident throughout the rest of the book: it is sufficient, for now, for you to have a basic grasp of the ideas and their potential application. It will be useful also, at this point, to ensure you recognise some of the origins and influences on the whole approach to the management of quality and the movement from industry to education of the various quality tools, as this will be a focus for the development of a critical review later in the book, drawing on the work of Bell (2003) and Coffield (2008).

The development of quality management as a policy and as a process

I wish all the men in my army were so regular like this shot.

(King George II)

It is important to note that the models of quality being applied within the service industry that is post-compulsory education today have their origins in manufacturing. It has been suggested that the development of quality assurance can best be exemplified by the production of lead shot for muskets between the sixteenth and eighteenth centuries.

These early firearms were notoriously unreliable, often jamming and exploding and causing injury to the user. One reason was the imperfections in musket balls and the lack of match to the dimensions of the barrel of the weapon. Having built his first shot tower in 1753, William Watts successfully patented a method for producing shot in *perfect globular form* in 1782 (Efstathios, 2010, page 9). Shot towers were constructed so that molten lead could be poured from a height through sieves with consistent dimensions of holes, with the result that the shot, cooling as it fell, was produced in a uniform and reliable shape.

What are the elements of quality assurance, evaluation and quality improvement here? Well, there was a need for assurance in the existing processes and products, a need to give the musketeers some level of confidence that their weapon would work safely. Over time there had been analysis and evaluation to see what could be done differently – Watts would not have been the first to try to solve the problem. There would have been trialling and testing of new systems and evaluation through the use of scrutineers of the final product to deem it 'fit for purpose' (although I doubt the men in Watts' employ used such a term). And so we see a simple but effective process established, one that demonstrably changed the quality of weaponry.

A leap forward to the second half of the twentieth century sees quality becoming a business science as well as a major element in advertising through reputation. Anyone over the age of 45 will probably remember their parents disparaging toys made in the Far East during the 1960s and early 1970s: 'made in Hong Kong' was a put-down not a plaudit. But, with the recent Toyota fall from grace notwithstanding, within 20 years manufacturers in Asia, particularly Japan, led in just about every field of manufacturing, from ocean-going liners to cars to MP3 players and, of course, toys. Both academics and employers would argue that it was the commitment to concepts of quality such as Total Quality Management (TQM) that was the driving force for this achievement.

We will now briefly highlight some of the best known names and some key ideas that have moved policy and practice of quality management forward in the second half of the twentieth century and which have most obviously informed the development of quality strategies within the post-compulsory sector.

The quality gurus

W. Edwards Deming was one who took the message of quality to Japan in the 1950s. He propounded a 14-point plan for the philosophy of management, with an emphasis on management responsibility for quality. Although not its author, Deming also promoted the Plan/Do/Check/Act cycle to encourage a systematic approach to problem solving.

Armand Feigenbaum was a contemporary of Deming, also working in Japan. He wrote the seminal text *Total Quality Control* in 1951, with the definition of total quality being, *an effective system for integrating quality development, quality maintenance and quality improvement efforts within an organisation...* (DTI, 2003, page 3). He deserves credit for moving the focus of quality from solely the manufacturing stage, by widening its scope, so that it would consider design and initial specification as well as delivery and any other functions that contributed to customer satisfaction.

Joseph Duran developed the quality trilogy: quality planning, quality control and quality improvement. His focus was on establishing and sustaining quality management through planning and through conserving success and repeating it, not allowing a successful project to deteriorate over time when energy and motivation moved on elsewhere.

A more recent guru, and one not relocating to Japan, was Philip Crosby. Crosby originated the concept of Zero Defects, arguing that 'good enough' won't do. He also proposed the notion that 'Quality is Free' (you might want to think about that) and that the quality professional must become more knowledgeable and communicative about their business. Crosby identified 'The Fourteen Steps to Quality Improvement', which included:

- make it clear that management is committed to quality;
- raise the quality awareness and personal concern of all employees;
- establish progress monitoring for the improvement process;
- encourage individuals to establish improvement goals for themselves and for their group;
- do it all over again to emphasise that the quality improvement process never ends.

Finally, Tom Peters' work has been mostly on leadership, particularly as a preferred alternative to management. One of his well-known concepts is 'Management by walking about', creating the opportunities for listening, teaching and facilitating within the organisation. It remains to be seen how most teachers in the sector would respond to their principal popping in to see what's happening, but I remember the head teacher in my primary school doing it all the time.

If you are from a manufacturing or management background, you may well be familiar with these figures and with the ideas and strategies. If you are not, please don't assume you will not benefit from further study. As will be argued later, not every concept or practice translates easily or effectively from industry to service settings. The better you understand the concepts and policies, the better you can stand up for yourself and justify your own strategies and outcomes, so we would commend further reading.

A very good source of detailed, easy-to-read and well-presented extracts about TQM can be found on the popular 'businessballs' website www.businessballs.com. Another valuable source is the Department for Trade and Industry (DTI) development package, *From Quality to Excellence* (DTI, 2003). (This is now archived as the DTI has become the Department for Business Innovation and Skills (BIS), but search engines will generate the document for you.)

From industry to education – the introduction of quality assurance within post-compulsory education

The development of 'quality management', 'quality teams', 'quality systems' and so on has been a feature of post-compulsory education for something like 20 years. Walkin's (1992) TQM-focused text, *Putting Quality into Practice*, provided an early statement of the potential within the sector and, in 1994, the North West Quality Network (an association of six FE colleges) published its *Quality Handbook*.

It was not that no one was not bothered about how good (or bad) post-compulsory education was before then, it was just that there was no nationally agreed formal framework, no widespread culture of quality management, no protocol and procedures to measure and improve the quality of teaching in the sector before that time. Further education, as it was commonly called, stood apart from schools, drew heavily on the professional experience of those teachers who were 'time-served' in industry and rather celebrated its distinctive nature. But it was common to find less than ideal practice.

Let me illustrate this with some case studies in the form of true stories.

CASE STUDY
The tale of the register

My first teaching post was at a small FE college in the North West of England.

I was teaching on the recently introduced City & Guilds 'Vocational Preparation Course'. It was my first appointment and the only paperwork required, other than producing some resources for the lessons, was to take a register. Having been shown the simple process of marking a '/' or a '0', I duly fulfilled my administrative duties for several weeks.

After a while I noticed that the number of '0s' was increasing. I was concerned as it seemed that more than one student had stopped attending altogether, while others were very erratic in their attendance. So I asked a colleague, ensconced in his regular staffroom armchair, what I should do about this. 'Don't worry,' he said, 'less marking for you to do'.

How would we balance such a response against today's drive for recruitment, retention and achievement, to say nothing of the simple professional concern for the young people involved? Well, we need to understand the context a little more, so here is another tale.

CASE STUDY
Another tale about registers

As recorded in the first tale, the keeping of the register did seem to be the only paperwork required in the early 1980s. However, one colleague was a little negligent about this, with the result that when his registers were required at the end of the year he had to, er ... how can I put this ... 'produce' them. He was skilful with assorted coloured pens, could produce convincing patterns of behaviour for best and worse attendees, had a knack of ageing the document with stains from the bottom of a coffee cup and completed the effect with a quick rub on the floor to gather some dust and create an aged patina.

[Two important points here: my colleague moved on a long time ago and the college is no more, so please put down the pen with which you were about to write to your MP/ newspaper and soothe your indignation.]

There is a point in the tale: the lack of importance attached to registers is explained by the fact that before Incorporation in 1993, colleges were funded by their Local Education Authority. (After Incorporation they became independent trusts and were funded directly via various government agencies.) The audit day was 1 November and monies for the year were allocated on the number of registered students on that date.

Apart from the obvious benefit of providing a roll-call in the event of fire, the only other main use for registers in those days was to inform exam/assessment entries in the spring (in those days there were no series of AS and A2 exams, no year-round roll-on-roll-off NVQs). There was a casualness in keeping registers that was not desirable but was, perhaps, understandable: once the money was received any changes in recruitment and retention had no effect on a college's financial operation so there was little incentive to vigorously monitor and manage students' attendance records. Remember that FE colleges were not in 'loco parentis', there wasn't the explicit duty of care because these were almost always adult learners and there was often a climate of 'well if they don't turn up that's their lookout'.

The casual approach to learners completing the course and achieving a qualification, as signified by the register losing some importance in the eyes of some colleagues after the audit date, may be the reason that, following Incorporation, one of the earliest changes in practice was to make funding dependent on the different elements of a student's experience. You will now find a strong focus on measures of registration, retention, achievement and success. This is something you are responsible for and for which your register is an essential record. Indeed, record keeping is now a specific LLUK Standard, AP 7.1, that must be successfully demonstrated in practice.

So there is an example of how practice has been changed and a quality assurance process – in the form of a professional standard – introduced. But this is just one: the actuality was that, following Incorporation, the sector was going to experience radical changes in management, curriculum and resourcing because the simple overall perception was that it was not doing a good job and that this was due in no small part to the culture, ethos and lack of accountability that was prevalent.

Incorporation provided the opportunity for a dramatic shift in the practice of stakeholders within the post-compulsory sector and subsequent impact on providers because funding became the lever through which change could be engineered. Once funding was not to be handed over on a set date it could be made dependent on a number of measures whose criteria were set by those holding the purse strings.

These various funding bodies have been:

- the Further Education Funding Council (FEFC) and the Training and Enterprise Councils (TEC), 1993–2001;
- the Learning and Skills Council (LSC), 2001–2010;
- the Young People's Learning Agency (YPLA) and the Skills Funding Agency (SFA), 2010–to date.

All have had a quality agenda, albeit executed in different ways, but it has always been predominantly target driven. In other words, if you want your money – and don't forget money equals jobs – then you will reach certain targets.

There have been various inspection regimes over the same time.

- FEFC, 1993–2001.
- Ofsted and the Adult Learning Inspectorate (ALI), 2002–2006.
- Ofsted, 2006–to date.

The focus, tools, intensity, duration and consequences of inspection have also evolved over time but, drawing on published reports critical of the quality of teaching and level of attainment within the sector, there has been a constant urge from the inspecting bodies for the sector to 'improve', see the general sector reports by Ofsted (2004a), Ofsted (2004b), and Ofsted (2008) for example.

Incorporation threw up many challenges and many changes. There was an aggressive approach to pay and conditions of service, many staff left, colleges were closed or merged, new management teams introduced. The opportunity to apply proven quality models (well proven in industry, let's say) to the new FE sector was very much of the moment and, with the approval of the FEFC, became a significant feature of the new inspection regime.

Now here is a salutary message for those readers who may be feeling they don't want to engage with all of this management of quality stuff.

I referred earlier to the North West Quality Network. One of our tasks had been to decide what was really important in influencing the overall quality of a learner's experience at a college and how could we measure performance against this to facilitate improvement where needed? An external consultant to the working party was the recently appointed leader inspector for the FEFC in the North West. We duly published our report and at a 'launch' event encouraged colleges to use the framework to measure how they were doing in advance of the anticipated FEFC inspections.

Well, it turned out that the FEFC were quite pleased with what we had come up with because much of their own inspection protocol, when published, was very familiar to those colleges in the working party or that had shown interest in the North West Quality Framework document. One consequence was that in the first round of inspection some of these colleges did much better than others, with beneficial consequences for their reputations and for their finances as they were funded by the FEFC to roll out 'best practice' to those colleges who had not performed so well. Now it may be that these were 'good' colleges anyway, but common sense suggests that if you have some insight into, and are prepared for, an external evaluation system it might be easier to do well than if you are in total ignorance. As we have indicated, the purpose of this book is to ensure you are both aware of the issues and confident with your own strategies – in other words, you embrace and use quality assurance and quality improvement to your advantage.

Where is quality assurance focused today?

I admit this is a major simplification of many years of development but we need to encourage you to begin to investigate and engage with the existing quality processes that are applied to the sector today and to which you will have to respond. We will visit, with some criticality, both past and current applications of some of the models of quality management, but for now, as we move towards the end of this introduction, we will signpost three important areas. These will provide a fundamental starting point and a minimum, but likely to be effective, foundation for your engagement with quality assurance and generate themes that the rest of this book will explore.

1. The Ofsted Common Inspection Framework, 2009 version

There's a whole chapter on this later but the five themes of the Common Inspection Framework (CIF) are:

- overall effectiveness;
- capacity to improve;
- outcomes for learners;
- quality of provision;
- leadership and management.

This is how colleges are judged and, as we will see later, the published judgements are powerful tools for both good and ill. Get a copy of the CIF and make sure you understand it. Do note that it has changed before and it will change again: if you peruse the work of the quality gurus you will find the clear philosophy that quality is continuous, not fixed.

2.The Framework for Excellence

Initiated by the LSC, and now the responsibility of the SFA, this document, and associated policies and procedures, stipulates those areas of work by which the effectiveness of a college is judged and future funding decisions are made. The Framework for Excellence (FfE) was developed in response to criticism of the unwieldy and complex nature of the bureaucracy surrounding evaluation of performance and associated funding issues that had developed within the LSC. There are some critics who would argue that the FfE hasn't achieved this, but that is a debate for elsewhere (see for example the responses from Edexcel (2006) and TUC (2008)). We will include it because it is a quality tool in use at the moment.

Category	Indicator
Learner and qualification success	Success rates
Learner views	Learner views
Learner destinations	Learner destinations
Responsiveness to employers	Employer views
	Amount of training
	Training Quality Standard
Financial health and management	Financial health
	Financial management and control evaluation
Resource efficiency	Funding per successful outcome

Table 1.1: Summary of Framework for Excellence

Overall, this is more obviously in the hands of management than individual teachers, but since it has a clear focus on learners and employers you will need to be able to account for the quality of what you do and be able to provide evidence to support judgements made by teams, departments and the whole college.

3. The Learning and Skills Improvement Service Excellence Gateway

The Learning and Skills Improvement Service (LSIS) was created in December 2007, effectively being a merger of the Quality Improvement Agency (itself only established in 2006) and the Centre for Excellence in Leadership (started in 2003). (Like I said, nothing is constant in this sector.) The LSIS is an invaluable site in that it provides resources on all aspects of the sector: on quality assurance and improvement; on continuing professional development, teaching and learning materials; exemplars of good practice; and guidance on preparation for inspection and much more.

In organising its resources for the 'learner journey' it provides an interesting framework for any teacher to consider and work within when addressing each and every aspect of their role and responsibility. The domains in which the quality-aware teacher will be active include:

- recruitment;
- initial assessment;
- induction;
- teaching, training, coaching and learning;
- learner support;
- assessment;
- reviewing learners' progress;
- retention;
- achievement;
- progression.

It looks like a tall order but these aspects are central to your role in the sector. It's certainly a lot more to be responsible for than a register...

A SUMMARY OF **KEY POINTS**

In this chapter we have:

> **considered what 'quality' means to us;**

> **identified some of the original thinkers – the 'quality gurus' – and early concepts and application of quality;**

> **defined the terms quality assurance, evaluation and quality improvement;**

> **looked at examples of quality assurance tools and processes within the sector;**

> **recognised some key areas of quality assurance in the sector: the Ofsted Common Inspection Framework, the Framework for Excellence and the LSIS Excellence Gateway.**

REFERENCES REFERENCES REFERENCES REFERENCES REFERENCES REFERENCES

Ball, S J (2003) The Teacher's Soul and the Terrors of Performativity. *Journal of Educational Policy,* 18 (2): 215–28.

Coffield, F (2008) *Just Suppose Teaching and Learning Became the First Priority...* London: Learning and Skills Network.

EdExcel Strategic Development Division (2006) *Policy Watch: Framework for Excellence: A Comprehensive Performance Assessment Framework for the Further Education System.*

Efstathios, T (2010) An Awkward Thing: Bristol's Lead Shot Tower. http://efstathios.co.uk/Historical/Shot_Tower_Standing/Essay_Tsolis_E.pdf (accessed July 2010).

LLUK (2007) *New Overarching Professional Standards for Teachers, Tutors and Trainers in the Lifelong Learning Sector*. London: LLUK.

Ofsted (2004a) *Why Colleges Succeed*. London: HMSO.

Ofsted (2004b) *Why Colleges Fail.* London: HMSO.

Ofsted (2008) *How Colleges Improve.* London: HMSO.

Praxiom (2010) *Quality Management Definitions*. www.praxiom.com/iso-definition.htm (accessed July 2010).

TUC (2008) *Framework for Excellence: A Comprehensive Performance Assessment Framework for the Further Education System*. www.unionlearn.org.uk/policy/learn-1073-f0.pdf

Walkin, L (1992) *Putting Quality into Practice*. Cheltenham: Stanley Thornes.

Websites

Businessballs www.businessballs.com

Department for Business, Innovation and Skills www.bis.gov.uk

Department for Education www.education.gov.uk

Institute for Learning www.ifl.org.uk

Learning and Skills Improvement Service ww.lsis.org.uk

Lifelong Learning UK www.lluk.org.uk

Office for Standards in Education (Ofsted) www.ofsted.gov.uk

Skills Funding Agency www.skillsfundingagency.com

Young People's Learning Agency www.ypla.gov.uk

2
Delivering quality in the classroom

This chapter is designed to:

- **provide you with a clear picture of how to deliver high quality lessons;**
- **develop your creativity;**
- **consider the Ofsted grading criteria and how to prepare for observed lessons;**
- **focus on how you can be consistent in delivering high quality lessons;**
- **discuss how you can benefit from sharing good practice with colleagues and how you can utilise and develop these skills in order to enhance your practice.**

It addresses the following Professional Standards for QTLS:

BK 1.3 Ways of creating a motivating learning environment.

CK 2.1 Ways to convey enthusiasm for own specialist area to learners.

DK 1.1 How to plan appropriate, effective, coherent and inclusive learning programmes that promote equality and engage with diversity.

It also addresses the Level 5 DTTLS module: Continuing personal and professional development.

Introduction

Teachers think of their students first.
Their cultural diversity is an intricate challenge.
Understanding their motivations helps to design the curriculum.
Knowing the students, their personalities and learning styles, helps to design the instruction.
What interests you, the teacher, is not unimportant, but cannot come first.
When you show your students that you care about them, they will return your interest with interest.

(Adapted from Nagel, 1998, page 31)

When considering the quality of teaching a good starting point is to define what we mean by an 'outstanding' teacher and why it is considered important in your teaching role.

When thinking of the word 'outstanding' what may spring to mind is 'being the best' or 'being perfect'. However, outstanding teachers are not perfect or infallible.

They are fallible, they make mistakes and they have lessons that do not always go as they expected. During this chapter we will use the word outstanding to mean 'grade 1' in the context of the current Ofsted grading criteria.

What makes teachers 'outstanding' is enthusiasm for their subject and their learners which facilitates genuine learning and attainment above what is expected. They will often have a reputation for delivering fun lessons where there is an excitement or 'buzz' for learning which enables the students to maximise their potential.

Quality lessons

When considering how to prepare and deliver quality lessons we will use the '5 Ps' model I have developed to use with my trainee teachers.

The 5 Ps to improving your practice are:

1. planning;
2. preparation;
3. personalisation;
4. professionalism;
5. proving it.

We will consider each of these and how it can help you to prepare and deliver 'outstanding' lessons.

Planning

When planning for learning we first need to consider the structure of the lesson and the time available.

If we use the analogy of a good meal, a meal in a top restaurant which you remember, enjoy and which enables you to experience something new and exciting, we can apply the same components of that experience to that of a lesson.

This structure includes six component parts and it is called the 'diet'. Each lesson we prepare should be prepared using this framework to ensure all the important areas are covered.

The structure should be:

Appetizer
A small bite-sized food served before a meal to whet one's appetite.

Plan a small appetizer before you start the lesson. A word search, quiz question or anagram could be used for students to complete while they are waiting for everyone to arrive and settle down. This will manage the noise and will encourage students to settle down and focus on the session from the very start. It also eliminates unstructured time and so helps to manage behaviour.

Starter
The first course of a meal.

Your starter activity should recap on previous learning and introduce the learning for the session. The aim of the starter is to 'warm up' the brain and to gently remind students of the progress they have made so far and to signpost the learning to come. Your starter activity should be short, sharp and snappy and should engage all the learners.

Research has shown that students learn more at the start and the end of sessions than in the middle, so it is vitally important to make use of this increased capacity to learn and to be creative and imaginative in the activities we choose to use.

Interactive quizzes, drag and drop exercises, cloudburst activities and small group tasks can be used to check previous learning and to focus learners on the lesson.

The main course
The pièce de résistance, or the centrepiece of the meal, is a culinary masterpiece or a dish fit for a king.

The main section needs to start with your aims and objectives being shared with the learners and being displayed throughout the lesson. Your aims and objectives should be differentiated and achievable within that lesson. See top tips below.

You need to keep the main section to a minimum. Remember that the attention span of a young person is their chronological age plus two in minutes. So, a 16-year-old can only be expected to concentrate for 18 minutes. Of course, this does not mean that for adults you can have main sections of 50 minutes, as the maximum adults can concentrate for is about 25 minutes!

When thinking about your main sections – and you may have more than one main section in a lesson, depending on the length of the lesson – remember that 80 per cent of your main section should be learning by doing or active learning and only 20 per cent should be teacher talk. So, if you are teaching a group of 18-year-olds, your main sections will be 20 minutes long, of which only six minutes should be teacher talk and 14 minutes should be taken up with the class learning by doing.

It is imperative that you make your six minutes of teacher input count. Make it interesting, focused and, most importantly, make it hard to forget. Using clips, animations and pictures can 'hook' the learners into your delivery and enable them to retain the key learning points by associating it with the 'hook'. Using mind maps, graffiti boards, music, colour or other accelerated learning techniques may enable learners to remember the learning by linking the left and right sides of the brain and increasing their capacity to learn. If you are interested in learning more about accelerated learning see the further reading at the end of this chapter.

The active learning component should involve the students in discovering information for themselves, discussing and presenting information, analysing information or creating information to share with others. By doing this we engage the cognitive domain and the higher levels of Bloom's taxonomy of learning, which are applying, analysing, evaluating and creating (Gould, 2009).

Dessert
The most important part of a meal – that rich gooey extra thing.

This is the part of the lesson we look forward to, where we check that learning has taken place, and we do this by using a wide variety of activities that engage and motivate learners and demonstrate the learning that has been achieved. Checking learning is also known as formative assessment. It is the informal monitoring and checking of understanding and the questioning of students to promote and confirm deep learning and not just surface under-standing.

Perfecting your questioning techniques is a key part of this. It is imperative that we use prompts and supplementary questions in order to extract the learning from the students. At the same time you will strongly encourage them to reflect on their learning and to analyse and evaluate its quality.

Varying your questioning techniques by using mini whiteboards, differentiated question cards, interactive quiz questions, sticky notes and getting students to write questions for each other will ensure that the students get used to answering questions and are comfor-table with the style of questioning you use.

It is important that you know your learners. Then you will adapt your questioning techniques to meet the needs of the individuals in that lesson. You do not treat them all the same, but you can demonstrate to your own satisfaction that each and every one of them has maxi-mised their learning in that session.

Cheese and biscuits
An additional course that finishes off the meal and is best served with a glass of port.

This is where summative assessment is used to formally assess the progress of our learners. We may not always have summative assessment built into our lessons, but throughout the scheme of work this type of assessment will be included in order to meet the requirements of the awarding body.

This may be in the form of final exams, coursework or portfolios of evidence, but can also be the completion of homework and activities undertaken in the lesson that are marked, and on which the learners receive feedback.

This feedback is vital in developing the potential of learners and in signposting them towards achieving the best result possible in their programme of study.

Coffee and mints
The last component that allows us to relax and leave with a smile.

This is your summary of the lesson and this is where you give learners a taste of what to expect next time. Try to whet their appetite by preparing them in advance for what you expect of them in the next lesson. It is important that you try to leave them with a smile on their faces. This is also your opportunity to ask for feedback on the lesson and how you can improve it in the future. We are often reluctant to ask learners what they think of our teaching, but we can derive so much from asking what worked for them. This will enable us to use this information to inform future planning and delivery.

PRACTICAL TASK PRACTICAL TASK PRACTICAL TASK PRACTICAL TASK PRACTICAL TASK

Take one of your lessons and plan it using the 'diet' framework.

Consider how easy it was. How different was it from what you normally do?

Rationale for planning

As you can see, planning lessons is a complex area and it is best to spend time getting this stage right before moving on to the preparation of resources, etc. Having a rationale for your choice of activities is very important. You need to be aware of current theory and be able to support your choice of structure and activities with clear reference to that theory.

If you do not have a separate rationale document to complete in your organisation then you should include it on your lesson plan. An example of this is one that refers to the possible assignment of separate roles within a specific activity and might read:

> *In group work the allocation of roles implies that each individual is an important part of the group and helps create a feeling of accountability. This promotes a sense of worth and belonging which is one of the important benefits of cooperative learning. Assigning roles provides explicit expectations and can add to the sense of order in the group work.*
>
> (Fogarty, 2002, page 192)

In light of this I have decided to allocate each person a specific role in the group work in today's lesson.

TOP TIPS TOP TIPS TOP TIPS TOP TIPS **TOP TIPS** TOP TIPS TOP TIPS TOP TIPS

Aims and objectives

- Aims are a general statement of intent – (one or a maximum of two per lesson).
- Objectives are specific, detailed and achievable statements, which lead to the general aims.
- Objectives should be differentiated – ('All learners will...' 'Most learners will...' 'Some learners will...').
- Aims and objectives should be shared with learners at the start of the lesson.
- Objectives should be checked at the end of the lesson to demonstrate achievement.
- Use words such as: 'state', 'describe', 'explain', 'list', 'evaluate', 'pick out', 'distinguish between', 'analyse', 'summarise', 'show diagrammatically', 'compare', 'apply', 'assess', 'suggest reasons why', 'give examples of', 'carry out', 'demonstrate'.
- Avoid words such as: 'know', 'understand', 'be familiar with', 'have a good grasp of', 'appreciate', 'be interested in', 'be aware of', 'believe'.
- Always start your objectives with the preface – 'By the end of this session, learners will be able to …'.
- Don't have too many objectives as you will have to show you have achieved them at the end of the session.
- The important thing is that your objectives are measurable – this means you can show that effective learning has taken place.

If we look at the current Ofsted grading standards the criteria of an outstandingly planned lesson are:

- *Highly detailed lesson plan – timing, structure and method. Excellent range of activities planned to meet different learning styles/needs.*
- *Comprehensive introduction – aims and objectives explained, shared and displayed. Learners demonstrate very clear understanding about learning purpose.*
- *Activities very well structured and timed to maintain interest and stimulate learning for all learners (buzz).*

You can see that the planning is essential to the achievement of a grade 1 outstanding lesson. Immaculate planning, preparation and presentation are the keys to being an outstanding teacher in the lifelong learning sector.

Preparation

Taking time to prepare activities and resources that are engaging and varied will pay dividends. If you think creatively and utilise a range of free resources you can produce a wide range of teaching and learning activities.

The presentation of your resources and handouts is vital. You must take extreme care to ensure they are easily understandable and free from errors.

TOP TIPS TOP TIPS **TOP TIPS** TOP TIPS **TOP TIPS** TOP TIPS **TOP TIPS** TOP TIPS

Preparing resources

- All resources should include a footer with your name and date on it and be free from errors and referenced appropriately.
- They should be prepared in a sans serif font – at least size 12 to allow dyslexic students to be able to read them.
- Handouts should be on pastel coloured paper to allow dyslexic students to be able to read them. You may get more specific guidance from learning support as some dyslexic people need a specific colour of paper.
- All images used should represent the diverse nature of the student group.
- Photocopies should be collated and stapled and should be easily readable.
- Activities should be well prepared and laminated where possible to preserve them for future use.
- You should check all activities before the session to ensure no bits are missing and check your technology before the lesson to make sure it is working.
- Always have a contingency plan in case the technology defeats you.
- Make sure all issues/topics are contemporary and relevant to the age range of your students.
- Carry a bag of tricks with pens, board markers, sticky notes, highlighters and flipchart paper. This will enable you to improvise if necessary and create activities on the spur of the moment if things go wrong.

Creativity is the process of finding and implementing new and appropriate ways of doing things. It is not necessary to be a 'creative' or 'artistic' person to be a creative teacher; you just need to be prepared to use the resources that are available and adapt them to suit your needs.

Variety is key to learning as none of us like to do the same thing over and over again. Many students complain today about 'death by PowerPoint' because many teachers use this as their only teaching technique. PowerPoint is an excellent tool to structure and focus a lesson but should be only a small component of the lesson and not the main focus.

Some of my favourite books for creative activities are:

50 Templates for Improving Teaching and Learning by Nigel Fisher
This book contains a CD-Rom with 50 templates you can adapt and use in the classroom. I particularly like the brain drops and the snowballing activities. A key strength of this text is that it also includes a rationale for each activity that is linked to theory.

The Creative Teaching and Learning Toolkit by Brin Best and Will Thomas
This book contains a CD-Rom with activities that supplement those outlined in the book. It clearly explains how to use each activity and what you need to prepare.

A Toolkit for Creative Teaching in Post-Compulsory Education by Linda Eastwood et al.
This book contains 50 activities that you can use in the classroom. It also includes a useful section about the danger points of each activity.

We Can Work It Out by Vickery and Spooner, the Association of Mathematics Teachers
This book contains activities you can photocopy to use as brain gym activities in any class-room or specifically in numeracy lessons.

For the full details of these books see further reading at the end of the chapter.

Other sources of free activities are the websites listed at the end of the chapter. These allow you to create activities such as word searches, crosswords, anagrams and domino games. Your interactive whiteboard also often has the software to enable you to prepare lots of these activities, including quizzes, puzzles and games.

It takes time to make resources and to get used to using the technology available, but they can be used in other sessions and kept for future years if you look after them.

Taking risks is part of the process of being a creative teacher and you may find that the technology does not always work as you had planned. As long as you have a back-up activity, this is fine. Students are very forgiving and they are prepared to give you credit for trying to make it more interesting for them.

PRACTICAL TASK PRACTICAL TASK **PRACTICAL TASK** PRACTICAL TASK **PRACTICAL TASK**

Using one of the sources mentioned above, create a new activity to use in one of your lessons.

- How did it go?
- How would you change it for next time?
- Will you try something similar again?
- If not, why not?

If we look at the current Ofsted grading standards the evidence for an outstandingly planned lesson is:

- *Excellent range/creative approaches used to maximise learning and involve learners. Highly appropriate for subject.*
- *All teaching and reference materials promote inclusion.*

You can see that being creative and innovative is a key requirement in the observation of lessons.

Personalisation

What we mean by personalisation is simply putting the learner at the centre of the process. Everything that we do as teachers should be to the benefit of that individual learner in the centre of their learning journey.

We know that the learner is at the centre of the learning journey with the teacher supporting them. Supplementary to this is the input of learning-support staff, the organisation, family and friends. All of these working together mean that the learner is likely to succeed on their own personal learning journey. Each learner is on a slightly different learning journey and, as such, will need different levels of support from the teacher and the people around them.

You may have in your classroom some very able students alongside those who are less able. It is important that each gets the support and level of work that is appropriate to their ability and that gives them enough challenge to push them to succeed, but not so much that it will be too hard and they will switch off. Making sure you meet the needs of all learners is called differentiation. Activities and objectives are differentiated to ensure all learners are able to learn at their own pace with sufficient challenge and positive outcomes.

TOP TIPS TOP TIPS TOP TIPS TOP TIPS **TOP TIPS** TOP TIPS TOP TIPS TOP TIPS

Differentiation

- At the start of every lesson visualise your weakest student, your average student and your strongest student. At the end, think 'Have I given them a good learning experience and have they all learned?'
- Ask yourself 'Do all students at varying levels make significant progress, become effective participants and achieve progression?'
- Vary activities but not for variety's sake! Use variety to match needs, raise, maintain and sustain motivation, enhance concentration and to reinforce new learning.
- Be aware of each individual's needs and plan to help them to learn.
- Make sure worksheets are accessible to everyone and build in extension activities for the more able.
- Use group work to support weaker students where appropriate.
- Set interesting and relevant projects that students can complete in a variety of different ways depending upon their learning style or ability.
- Use individual target-setting to monitor progress and to allow students to work at a pace that is challenging but achievable for them.
- Put your students at the heart of the learning.
- Challenge all students but don't set them impossible tasks – some students may work to the pass criteria while some will work to the distinction criteria – but all will pass!

PRACTICAL TASK PRACTICAL TASK PRACTICAL TASK PRACTICAL TASK PRACTICAL TASK

Prepare a set of questions for a group of learners using:

- Which? questions for evaluation;
- How? questions for synthesis;
- Why? questions for analysis.

Did learners demonstrate deeper understanding?

If we look at the Ofsted grading standards (Appendix 2) the evidence for an outstandingly planned lesson is:

- *Highly effective range of assessment techniques used to check all learners' knowledge and progress throughout. Progress and achievements recorded and evaluated regularly with the learner.*
- *Outstanding standards of work. All learners demonstrating excellent knowledge and skills.*

You can see that the checking that learning has taken place is fundamental in confirming the learning experience and providing evidence for the observation of teaching and learning.

CASE STUDY

Observations – by Alex – Curriculum Quality Manager

My role is to raise the quality of teaching and learning across the college and a major part of this is the observation of teaching. Last year I observed 158 lessons in all areas of the college. The five key things I am looking for are:

1. Is learning taking place throughout the lesson?
2. Is there a good relationship between learners and teacher that encourages participation and inclusion?
3. Is there a good level of challenge in the lesson – are **all** learners being pushed to achieve?
4. Are the learners actively learning?
5. Is the lesson well planned and resourced?

The focus of observations has changed recently from a focus on the paperwork, schemes of work and lesson plans, to a focus on the learning.

Schemes of work and lesson plans are still important quality documents but they are a very small part in deciding if a lesson is outstanding or not.

The best way I can describe a grade 1 lesson is that it *feels* like a grade 1. From the minute you walk into the room you get a feeling of learning taking place, of excitement and enjoyment. Learners are actively involved throughout the lesson and are clearly able to articulate what they have done, why they have done it and how doing it takes them closer to their learning goals.

This feeling is underpinned by impressive levels of planning, preparation and paperwork.

We can see from this case study that the observation of teaching and learning is a key focus for all Post-Compulsory Education and Training (PCET) organisations and plays a major part in the quality assurance systems of the organisation.

CASE STUDY

Advanced Practitioners – by Jane Martin – Shrewsbury College

In March 2004, the Learning and Skills Development Agency published a report, *From Little Acorns: Towards a Strategy for Spreading Good Practice Within Colleges* (Cox and Smith, 2004). The report found that good practice in further education colleges often remained hidden or unexploited because staff lacked the strategies and skills to share such practice in their organisations. The ten recommendations resulting from the study included the appointment of 'knowledge brokers' or Advanced Practitioners (APs) to facilitate the transfer of good practice.

Shrewsbury College responded to the challenge of continuing a college-wide improvement in teaching and learning, and implemented the recommendation by appointing three APs. Central to the role was the drive to improve the quality of teaching and learning throughout the college.

This was achieved by the development of innovative strategies; dissemination of best practice; support and mentoring of staff; promotion of effective use of ILT across the college; and the design and delivery of training.

This was an exciting initiative. Initially, the role focused on three separate projects: behaviour management, e-ILPs and a VLE-based tutorial system. Collaborative work to improve the quality and consistency of tutorials provided the opportunity to explore ways in which the Personal Tutor role could be more effectively implemented. A college-wide scheme of work was designed and introduced, together with session plans and resources, all of which could be altered to meet the needs of different learners. The feedback from staff was very positive and prompted suggestions for further improvements.

The college had already established a mentoring system within departments, but a significant aspect of the APs' role was to support and mentor newly appointed staff and those on Initial Teacher Training courses.

In practice, this extended to members of staff who wanted to develop and extend their skills in order to improve the quality of their practice. This has remained a consistent part of our work as APs, and it is often the most rewarding. It facilitates the transfer of good practice and addresses barriers to professional development at a personal level.

One-to-one mentoring was complemented by a system of twilight training sessions which was introduced in order to respond to issues which arose from lesson observations. The process of observation has been a valuable mechanism for validating good practice and addressing individual development needs. However, this formal approach has been enriched by the implementation of a system of peer observation throughout the college. As APs, we were closely involved in the development of policy and practice, both of which have been revised and improved.

This year, members of staff were encouraged to make links with colleagues outside their subject area. Early indications are that this latest development has enhanced the process, thus providing further evidence of the valuable impact of active and collaborative approaches to the sharing of good practice. A report summarising the observation reports is presented to the management team; this provides a useful guide to the design and implementation of a programme of training events, which are provided throughout the year.

The teaching and learning strategy developed by the college has provided a clear and coherent strategy towards continuous improvement. Geoff Petty's involvement led to a series of programme-based, experimental initiatives led by members of staff and supported by APs. The positive impact on staff and students provided an impetus to further innovation and experimentation, the results of which were shared with colleagues at the annual Teachers' Conference in September.

As colleagues have continued to embrace new ideas and practice. The role of the APs is changing again to support and develop college strategy, and the personal and professional development of a team of learning coaches. Training provided by the Learning and Skills Improvement Service (LSIS) has proved invaluable in providing resources and guidance towards achieving Advanced Learning Coach (ALC) status.

This will facilitate the introduction of coaching to improve teaching, training and learning. The role will also provide a focal point for learning coaches and explore strategies to embed and sustain them in the college.

One of the most rewarding aspects of the AP role has been the opportunity to participate in a process that has undoubtedly improved the quality of teaching and learning in the college, and that has unlocked potential for both teachers and students alike.

A SUMMARY OF **KEY POINTS**

In this chapter we have:

> explored the 5 Ps to improve your practice;

> discussed the role of creativity in engaging the learner in the process;

> considered judgements made by Ofsted in grading lessons and how they relate to the 5 Ps;

> identified strategies that will enable you to become an 'outstanding' teacher.

REFERENCES REFERENCES REFERENCES REFERENCES REFERENCES REFERENCES

Best, B and Thomas, W (2007) *The Creative Teaching and Learning Toolkit.* London: Continuum.

Cox, P and Smith, V (2004) *From Little Acorns: Towards a Strategy for Spreading Good Practice Within Colleges.* London: Learning and Skills Development Agency.

Gould, J (2009) *Learning Theory and Classroom Practice in the Lifelong Learning Sector.* Exeter: Learning Matters.

Fisher, N (2007) *50 Templates for Improving Teaching and Learning.* Lewes: Connect Publications.

Fogarty, R. (2002) *Brain Compatible Classrooms (2nd ed).* London: Corwin Press.

Nagel, G (1998) *The Tao of Teaching.* New York: Plume.

Ofsted (2004) *Framework for the Inspection of Initial Training of Further Education Teachers.* HMI 2274. London: Ofsted Publications.

FURTHER READING FURTHER READING **FURTHER READING** FURTHER READING

You might like to read the following books:

Robson, J (2008) *Teacher Professionalism in Further and Higher Education*. London: Routledge.
   This book focuses on professionalism, professional standards and the nature of professionalism within the workplace. It provides an interesting overview of the developments within the industry and the role of teachers within it.

Wallace, S (2007) *Teaching, Tutoring and Training in the Lifelong Learning Sector* (3rd ed). Exeter: Learning Matters.
   This book is good because it focuses on specific issues that occur in the lifelong learning sector and is full of useful hints and tips. This is particularly helpful for people new to teaching.

Also:

Best, B and Thomas, W (2007) *The Creative Teaching and Learning Toolkit*. London: Continuum.

Eastwood, L et al. (2009) *A Toolkit for Creative Teaching in Post-Compulsory Education*. Maidenhead: Open University Press.

Ginnis, P (2002) *The Teacher's Toolkit*. Camarthen: Crown House.

Fisher, N (2007) *50 Templates for Improving Teaching and Learning*. Lewes: Connect Publications.

Smith, A (2003) *Accelerated Learning – A User's Guide*. Bodmin: MPG Books Ltd.

Vickery, A and Spooner, M (2004) *We Can Work It Out*. Derby: Association of Teachers of Mathematics.

Websites

Brain box www.brainboxx.co.uk
Hot potatoes www.hotpotato.com
Puzzle maker www.puzzlemaker.com
Puzzle–maker www.puzzle-maker.com

3
External inspection

This chapter is designed to:

- provide you with a clear picture of the existing external inspection process;
- develop your understanding of the need for external inspection;
- consider the role of Ofsted in inspecting the sector;
- focus on how you can be prepared for external inspection.

It addresses the following Professional Standards for QTLS:

AS 4 Reflection and evaluation of their own practice and their continuing professional development as teachers.

AS 6 The application of agreed codes of practice and the maintenance of a safe environment.

It also addresses the Level 5 DTTLS module: Continuing personal and professional development.

Introduction

Wise teachers give students long reins.
They realise that under light pressure, growing gradually,
students will be less likely to weary of the burden of learning new ideas.
(Adapted from Nagel, 1998, page 31)

In industry, companies are required to have an independent audit of their financial and business performance every year. The results of this audit are published and are available to all of the stakeholders of the business and to anyone thinking of getting involved with that business.

The process of external inspection in the lifelong learning sector performs a similar function. In order to provide independent feedback to stakeholders and prospective stakeholders on the performance of an organisation there needs to be a process of 'auditing' carried out. This process of external inspection changes often, but the intention is always the same. It is to ensure that stakeholders are getting value for money and high quality provision and that the organisation is able to monitor its own performance and make necessary improvements.

The quality assurance system for post-16 education and training provision

In November 2010, the government department for Business, Innovation and Skills (BIS) produced its framework entitled *The Quality Assurance System for Post-16 Education and Training Provision.*

This framework sets out how education and training providers, local authorities, agencies and government departments are expected to work together to ensure that provision is high quality and meets or exceeds national standards.

What this means for providers of post-16 education and training

Although a number of organisations will have an interest in a particular provider, each provider will be held to account for the quality of its provision by a single sponsoring body.

- School sixth forms will be the responsibility of the home local authority.
- Sixth Form Colleges will be the responsibility of the home local authority supported by guidance issued by the YPLA.
- FE colleges will be the responsibility of the SFA.
- Providers of apprenticeships will be the responsibility of the National Apprenticeship Service (NAS), working on behalf of the SFA.

All post-16 education and training providers will have annual performance assessments with their sponsoring body. This will provide the opportunity for providers and sponsoring bodies to discuss the providers' assessment of how they are performing, taking into account the outcomes of Ofsted inspections and comparative benchmarking information from Framework for Excellence. The role of the sponsoring body is to provide support, challenge and, where necessary, to intervene so that poor performance is addressed quickly and robustly.

A provider that secures positive outcomes for its learners, has effective governance and sound financial health can expect little challenge from their sponsoring body. Conversely, a sponsoring body will pay greater attention to a provider where there are issues or concerns about their performance or financial position.

Providers and sponsoring agencies need routinely to collect and analyse evidence and data about their services and the outcomes they deliver for learners and employers. Providers will use this to:

- identify areas of good practice for sharing with other institutions or practitioners;
- review and reflect on current practice to see where improvements can be made;
- provide the public with an honest assessment of value for money.

Sponsoring bodies will use this to:

- make better informed commissioning and contracting decisions;
- target support to providers who are underperforming;
- undertake statutory intervention where there are significant concerns about the performance of an institution.

Most importantly, having access to the right information enables learners (and in many cases their parents, carers or employers) to make informed decisions about what and where they want to learn (BIS, 2010). This framework clearly lays down the roles and responsibilities of all the agencies involved in the sector and the process that they will follow to monitor the performance of providers. One of the key players in monitoring the quality of provision will be Ofsted.

Ofsted

Ofsted is the Office for Standards in Education, Children's Services and Skills. It regulates and inspects on behalf of the government to achieve excellence in the care of children and young people, and in education and skills for learners of all ages.

Ofsted inspects a wide range of further education and training providers, and will compare standards across the range of publicly funded provision. It is responsible for those organisations currently funded by local authorities on behalf of the DCSF and BIS including:

- education and training for 14–19-year-olds in a local area;
- all work-based learning (provided wholly or partly on employers' premises) for people aged 16 or over – for example, apprenticeships and national vocational qualifications;
- education for people aged 19 or over in FE colleges, local authorities or voluntary organisations;
- work-based and adult learning in prisons and young offenders' institutions, at the invitation of Her Majesty's Chief Inspector of Prisons.

Ofsted also inspects organisations funded by other government departments including:

- training for employment funded by the Department for Work and Pensions (DWP), including the New Deals;
- training of men and women from the armed services for the Ministry of Defence (MoD).

At the present time, an inspection of a further education organisation is carried out under the Education and Inspection Act 2006. It is a process of evidence-gathering in order to provide an evaluation of how well a college or provider is performing.

Inspections are short and focused, and dialogue with senior managers in the college or provider plays a central part. The provider's self-assessment provides the starting point for inspectors, and the views of learners, employers and other stakeholders are taken into account.

Inspections are conducted by an inspection team. The size of the team is determined by the number of learners, the geographical spread, and the range of the provision. Inspections result in a written report indicating one of four grades for the college's or provider's overall effectiveness in meeting the needs and interests of learners and other users. These are:

- outstanding;
- good;
- satisfactory; or
- inadequate.

The frequency of inspections is in proportion to risk.

Ofsted inspects colleges and providers using the Common Inspection Framework for further education and skills 2009.

When do inspections take place?

From September 2009, Ofsted has varied the frequency of college and provider inspections, depending on the outcome of an annual process for selecting providers for inspection. This involves reviewing their previous inspections and their subsequent performance.

Colleges and providers that were satisfactory at their last inspection will be inspected within four years of that inspection. These providers may receive a monitoring visit between inspections to check on progress.

Colleges or providers judged inadequate at their last inspection will continue to receive monitoring visits, followed by a full or partial reinspection approximately 12–15 months after the previous one.

Good or outstanding colleges or providers may have up to six years between inspections unless there are concerns about their performance or other aspects of their provision. Good or outstanding colleges or providers not inspected within three years of their last inspection will receive an assessment of their performance, called an interim assessment. This assessment will draw on performance data on all aspects of their provision and a published letter will inform the college or provider that it will not be inspected in that academic year.

How much notice do colleges and providers get of an inspection?

Colleges and providers will receive between two and three weeks' notice of an inspection. Ofsted may arrange for any college or provider to be inspected without notice where there are particular reasons, such as concerns about safeguarding or a rapid decline in performance. Monitoring visits will be conducted with three weeks' notice.

How are learners and employers involved?

Ofsted will ask colleges and providers to inform all their learners and employers about the inspection and Ofsted will pass on a message via email, inviting them to provide their views directly to the inspection team. This will be done shortly after notice of inspection up until the first day of the inspection. The email suggests topics that learners and employers may want to comment on to inspectors. These include the quality of teaching, learning and assessment, the effectiveness of the care, guidance and support they receive, and how well the provision meets their individual needs.

Inspectors will talk to learners to find out their views about the organisation and what it provides for them. They will also visit or telephone learners and employers at work.

When is the inspection report published?

The inspection report is published within 25 working days of the inspection. It includes a summary report for learners and employers that contains the main findings.

The Ofsted experience

The Learning and Skills Development Agency (LSDA) produced a report in 2003 called *Stories From the Front Line: the Impact of Inspection on Practitioners*. The report investigated the experiences of a number of practitioners and their experiences of the Ofsted inspection process. Although the report was focused on a slightly different inspection regime to the current one, the experiences are still valid and some of these are shared below:

Six weeks before the inspection there was a relatively small amount of preparation activity reported – for example a few briefing sessions and some memos. There was still an atmosphere of fairly routine normality. By the time practitioners found themselves four weeks away from the inspection anxiety, stress and pressure were building up. There was a short burst of confidence at the time of the inspection consultant's visit, but soon afterwards the practitioners experienced more pressure and some reported feeling depressed at the prospect of an inspection. Just before inspection this depression moved into a period of manic activity.

During the inspection week itself some practitioners experienced very rapid emotional ups and downs, depending on how much contact they had with inspectors. Some were described as swinging rapidly from panic and hysteria to deflation or from nervous anticipation to disappointment within the course of a day. Emotions were strongly felt and there were reports of colleagues feeling indignant, sidelined or crying.

For those practitioners who viewed inspection as a battlefield, the preparation for the inspection had many of the trappings of preparation for war. Money was spent on new resources e.g. information technology (IT), but because these had to be rushed through there was little time to make sure they were appropriate or that practitioners knew how to use them.

Some of the 'front-line troops' regularly used irony and humour, albeit sometimes a gallows humour, to keep up morale. The inspectors were identified as the enemy and the college members were described as banding together in a spirit of camaraderie and loyalty to the college.

The result of this approach was two-fold. On the one hand morale was kept relatively high during inspection but on the other hand weak practices and practitioners were hidden from inspectors. The practitioners experienced the pre-inspection period as a preparation to be under siege. This may have been because they saw the FE sector as a whole as being underfunded and under attack.

It may have been that they felt that their particular college was under threat following the recent, rapid changes in funding and inspection regimes.

The grades their college received mattered to them. One diary-keeper reported that in their college poor grades had led to redundancies in one section. Another diary-keeper was worried whether the poor grades they had received would adversely affect recruitment of both students and staff. She wondered whether or not she would be able to find another job once it became known that she had worked for a 'failing college'. In a college where practitioners expected good grades, they expressed feelings of shock and defeat when they received poor grades in the end. In this college the post-inspection de-briefings led by senior managers were described as 'Nuremburg trials'.

The 'battleground' for inspections is a shifting one. During these shifts senior managers responded to their lack of knowledge and reliable information by over-preparing for inspection. They put more and more pressure on their captains in the field (middle managers) and their ground troops (teachers) to invent and produce large quantities of paperwork as ammunition to counter what they perceived as an inspection attack. This scattergun technique was seen as effective because managers believed that the colleges that got the best grades were the ones that had produced the most paperwork.

For some practitioners inspection had an image of theatre and they behaved as if they and their college were taking part in a show with an audience of inspectors. This theatre image led them to feel either cynical or ambivalent about the accuracy of any conclusions reached by the inspectors.

At some point, in every college studied, inspection was planned and rehearsed for as if it were a show. All the main features of a show were present – there were auditions, scripts, rehearsals and a 'dress rehearsal' in the form of a mini-inspection with a consultant. New 'props' were provided and there was an audience (inspectors) who were not expected to know what was going on back stage.

In one college, Self Assessment Reports (SARs) were re-written by senior managers and their contents read and learnt by middle managers as if they were a script.

In theory, the Self Assessment Reports produced in each section should have given each manager and each course tutor an understanding of how effective their provision was and helped them to make plans for the future. In practice, SARs were seen as resulting from an externally imposed system that had to be complied with to achieve future funding. It was described as difficult and stressful for these middle managers to learn a script when they did not believe in or understand the content. The understanding and use of benchmarks highlights this. Senior managers expected middle managers to be able to discuss their course data in relation to 'national benchmarks'. However, the middle managers were unsure which benchmarks to use and even where they did know this, they were sceptical about the validity of comparing their performance with other, completely different colleges.

In conclusion the report stated that:

The image of inspection in all the colleges was that of a battlefield or theatre rather than of a consultancy. This image affected practitioners negatively and influenced their expectations of the outcomes of inspection. Senior managers, in their approach to preparing for inspections, further reinforced these images, rather than using inspection as an opportunity for promoting self-evaluation and reflection. The cultures of the colleges varied but none of them appeared to be based on the notion of collegiality or on the ethic of continuous improvement.

Sickness, stress and increased staff turnover were reported in all cases during and as a result of the inspection process. In the short term, the inspection experience did not seem to fulfil the function of improving teaching and learning. The grades that colleges received did not reflect the reality of the college experience for these practitioners and there was little evidence to show that colleges generally used them from one inspection to another to help improve their practice. The content of this report demonstrated that it was not just the large amounts of extra work that stressed teachers so much as the expectation that they should compromise their integrity and their commitment to teaching by producing what they saw as unnecessary and invented paperwork. Inspection will continue to be a stressful experience for practitioners until a culture of self-evaluation and continuous improvement is embedded at all levels and all sections within the college.

(Extracted from: LSDA (2003) *Stories From the Front Line – the Impact of Inspection on Practitioners.* www.lsnlearning.org.uk)

PRACTICAL TASK PRACTICAL TASK **PRACTICAL TASK** PRACTICAL TASK **PRACTICAL TASK**

- Talk to members of staff in your organisation about their experiences of Ofsted inspections.
- Do they have similar experiences to those identified by LSDA?
- Have you had experience of an Ofsted inspection? If so, what are your feelings?

CASE STUDY

My own experiences of Ofsted

During my 20 years working in the sector I have experienced six Ofsted inspections in various organisations and with varying levels of involvement with the inspection process. My first experience as a brand new teacher was very positive. It seemed that inspectors could give very positive feedback. They observed three times in one week, and appreciated my preparation and confident use of colour acetates, which were deemed to be effective from the front of the classroom. The emphasis appeared to be on my preparation and my delivery and not on the students themselves.

Over the years this has changed. Ofsted now focuses on the impact of the teaching on the learning of the students and their success on the programme and beyond.

In my most recent experience of Ofsted in a college I was very involved as a quality manager in the preparation for the visit and the management of the process. This required me to undertake a series of joint observations of staff with an Ofsted inspector. This was daunting as they were judging my ability to grade lessons in order that they could have confidence in the college's system of observing teaching and learning.

Very few actual observations of lessons took place, which was disappointing for staff who had spent many hours getting ready and would have valued the opportunity to contribute to the process. However, one unfortunate trainee teacher was observed three times in the week out of a total of 26 observations across the whole college! This was very unlucky as he was picked at random for his subject area, for tutorials and for key skills by different inspectors.

My feeling about the process as it exists at present is that it is a little too 'light touch'. Staff, students and stakeholders would probably value a more comprehensive audit of provision in order that they can have confidence in the findings and feel that it is a true reflection of the organisation's full range of capabilities.

Framework for Excellence

The Framework for Excellence (FfE) is the government's performance assessment framework for colleges and other providers. The FfE will provide public, comparable information for all post-16 education and training providers from 2012. This will give the public, and learners and employers in particular, better information about the quality of post-16 provision offered by different institutions and providers. Once the FfE has been fully implemented, we expect the assessment of providers' performance against the agreed minimum standards to be based largely on FfE information. The FfE will also provide important benchmarking information to help providers with their self-assessments.

It works by bringing together and recording provider achievement in three key areas of performance: responsiveness, effectiveness and finance. Each area has two or three key performance areas and these, in turn, are measured by a number of performance indicators (see Table 3.1).

The FfE focuses on:

- finance;
- learners and employer responsiveness;
- effectiveness.

Whereas inspection focuses on:

- quality of teaching and learning;
- learner support and guidance;
- leadership and management;
- achievement and standards.

The aim is for these two systems to complement each other and to provide different sorts of feedback to the organisations. All providers will use the framework as a basis for self-assessment and to refer explicitly to the framework's performance indicators in the self-assessment reports.

This is a new initiative and has yet to prove its effectiveness in raising standards in the sector.

Dimension	Key performance area	Performance indicators
Responsiveness	• Responsiveness to learners	• Learner views • Learner destinations
	• Responsiveness to employers	• Employee views • Amount of training • Training Quality Standard Accreditation
Effectiveness	• Quality of outcomes	• Qualifications success rates
	• Quality of provision	• Inspection grade
Finance	• Financial health • Financial management and control • Use of resources	• Financial health • Financial management and control • Funding economy • Resource efficiency • Capital

Table 3.1: Key performance areas and performance indicators needed to calculate overall performance rating

IQER

The Quality Assurance Agency for Higher Education's (QAA) role is to ensure that there is a high standard of higher education qualifications in the country and to inform and encourage continuous improvement in the management of the quality of higher education. In order to do this, QAA undertakes reviews of higher education provision delivered in further education colleges on behalf of the Higher Education Funding Council for England (HEFCE), which has statutory responsibility for ensuring that provision is made for assessing the quality of education provided by institutions it funds. From 2007–08 the process of review used in colleges in England has been the Integrated Quality and Enhancement Review (IQER). The IQER involves monitoring the management of the student learning experience and the college performance of its responsibilities based on the academic standards and quality of its higher education provision.

Colleges do not currently have powers to award higher education qualifications, although as we go to press the current government is reviewing this. It is likely to make changes to allow colleges to award their own higher education qualification. Currently, colleges work with awarding bodies, in particular Edexcel and/or one or more higher education institutions. The awarding bodies retain responsibility for the academic standards of all awards granted in their names and for ensuring that the quality of learning opportunities offered through collaborative arrangements is at least sufficient to enable students to achieve the academic standard required for their awards.

The IQER focuses on how colleges discharge their responsibilities within the context of their agreements with awarding bodies. The overarching aims of the IQER are to:

- support colleges in evaluating and improving their management of their higher education, for the benefit of students, and within the context of their agreements with awarding bodies;
- foster good working relationships between colleges and their awarding bodies, for the benefit of students;
- enable HEFCE to discharge its statutory responsibility for ensuring that provision is made for assessing the quality of education provided by the institutions it funds;
- provide public information.

The IQER usually takes place in two complementary stages called developmental engagement and summative review. The emphasis of the developmental engagement is on supporting the college in developing its higher education provision and its management of the student learning experience in an open and collegial way. The summative review is primarily concerned with reviewing, and making judgements about, the effectiveness of the college's procedures for the management of the student learning experience and their implementation.

Both stages of the IQER:

- focus on a college's management of the student learning experience for its higher education provision;
- acknowledge the shared responsibilities of awarding bodies and colleges, and seek to enhance these relationships;
- are based on a self-evaluation prepared by the college.

CASE STUDY
My reflections on the IQER process

The IQER process is relatively new and most organisations are just undertaking their first summative reviews. My only direct experience of a developmental review was found to be a very interesting process.

The need to get awarding institutions to attend and input into the process is difficult for colleges to manage. Also, each awarding institution has vastly different procedures and policies. Bringing all of that together and finding common strengths can be a difficult process.

The main thing we learnt was the need to work together across the organisation and to share good practice. We set up an HE working group and regularly met to share our developments on issues such as assessment and grading. We also set up a forum for students on HE courses to share their experiences and to contribute to the planning of programmes.

One of the positive outcomes of this was the setting up of a HE area for mature students to socialise and relax rather than being mixed in with the general student body.

As teachers working on HE courses we were used to following the quality assurance mechanisms of the awarding body but had not worked together to standardise the experience for students across the variety of different courses.

We can see from the discussions in this chapter that there is a need and a desire for external inspection. However, what it looks like and how it will change in the future will be dependent on the political situation and the needs and wants of the various stakeholders that exist in the sector.

The best thing you can do is be prepared at all times for some form of inspection. I have learnt from long and sometimes bitter experience that keeping your teaching files, lesson plans and schemes of work up to date is the easiest way of being prepared. Developing high quality lessons and resources that can be used repeatedly is another form of preparedness.

The main value of this preparedness is that you will establish a reputation for good planning, preparation and delivery and this will feed forward in to positive feedback from learners and good results for analysis.

If you do this, nothing can catch you unawares and you will feel a lot less stressed when you get the notification that Ofsted is on its way.

PRACTICAL TASK PRACTICAL TASK PRACTICAL TASK PRACTICAL TASK PRACTICAL TASK

Find out if your organisation delivers higher education programmes.

If they do, have a look at their IQER report – what does it say about the quality of provision?

A SUMMARY OF **KEY POINTS**

In this chapter we have:

> considered the role of external inspection in the sector;

> discussed the functions of Ofsted, the IQER and the FfE;

> considered the impact of external inspection on practitioners;

> identified strategies that will enable you to prepare for external inspection.

REFERENCES REFERENCES REFERENCES REFERENCES REFERENCES REFERENCES

BIS (2010) *The Quality Assurance System for Post-16 Education and Training Provision.* www.bis.gov.uk

LSDN (2003) *Stories From the Front Line: the Impact of Inspection on Practitioners.* www.lsnlearning.org.uk

Nagel, G (1998) *The Tao of Teaching*. New York: Plume.

FURTHER READING FURTHER READING FURTHER READING FURTHER READING

You might like to read the following books:

Bostock, J and Wood, J (2011) *14–19 Education – A Guide Book*. Maidenhead: Open University Press. This book focuses on the full role of the teacher in this very demanding sector including the role of quality assurance and evaluation.

Scales, P (2008) *Teaching in Lifelong Learning.* Maidenhead: Open University Press. This book is good because it focuses on specific issues that occur in the lifelong learning sector and is full of useful hints and tips. This is particularly helpful for people new to teaching.

Also:

Lea, J, Hayes, D, Armitage, A, Lomas, L and Markless, S (2003) *Working in Post-Compulsory Education.* Maidenhead: Open University Press.

Race, P (2005) *Making Learning Happen – A Guide for Post-Compulsory Education.* London: Sage Publications.

Rogers, J (2007) *Adults Learning* (5th ed). London: Open University Press.

Websites

Department for Business, Innovation and Skills www.bis.gov.uk

Framework for Excellence www.skillsfundingagency.bis.gov.uk

IQER www.qaa.ac.uk/reviews/iqer

LSDA www.lsnlearning.org.uk

Ofsted www.ofsted.gov.uk

4
Internal inspection

This chapter is designed to:

- **provide you with a clear understanding of the role of internal inspection in the lifelong learning sector;**
- **discuss the increased reliance on self-regulation;**
- **consider the observation of teaching and learning in the lifelong learning sector;**
- **focus on how you can prepare for internal inspection in your organisation.**

It addresses the following Professional Standards for QTLS:

AS 7 Improving the quality of their practice.

AP 5.1 Communicating and collaborating with colleagues and/or others, within and outside the organisation, to enhance learners' experience.

It also addresses the Level 5 DTTLS module: Continuing personal and professional development.

Introduction

> *Water is fluid, soft and yielding, but water will wear away rock,*
> *which is rigid and cannot yield.*
> *As a rule, whatever is fluid, soft and yielding will overcome*
> *whatever is rigid and hard.*
> *The wise leader knows that yielding overcomes resistances,*
> *and gentleness melts rigid defences.*
>
> (Adapted from Heider, 1985, page 155)

The responsibility for quality and improvement lies within colleges and providers themselves. Each organisation knows what is best for it and where its strengths and weaknesses lie. The pursuit of excellence calls for a strong and enduring commitment on the part of individual organisations to monitor and improve their own performance.

The aim of the government and its national partners is to support the efforts of individual colleges and providers to improve by:

- regular and open assessments of their performance and quality;
- managing and improving their performance;
- developing over time the capacity for self-regulation by the sector.

The first step in achieving excellence is to have reliable, easily understood, publicly available information on performance. Colleges, providers and national agencies need to have a robust and consistent basis for identifying performance and quality. They can then assess how their current provision matches this.

PRACTICAL TASK PRACTICAL TASK PRACTICAL TASK PRACTICAL TASK PRACTICAL TASK

PRACTICAL TASK PRACTICAL TASK PRACTICAL TASK PRACTICAL TASK **PRACTICAL TASK**

Identify the different procedures that exist in your own organisation to monitor the quality of their provision.

- Do they work?
- What do the staff think?

CASE STUDY

Lorraine Roberts, newly qualified teacher

As a recently qualified teacher one of the factors that influence my teaching practice is the notion of quality within teaching. When trying to investigate the role of quality within my role, I searched to find policy documentation and information on the impact of this phenomenon within my college. After much investigation, taking advice from colleagues and soul searching I was advised that it is 'embedded in everything we do'. I found this a little unhelpful and quite ambiguous.

As the influences of quality are embedded within all aspects of college life, quite often you will notice, particularly in terms of the inspection process, that 'things' outside of your control can impact hugely on your teaching practice.

Quality within teaching is judged not only on your performance, whether the class seem engaged, or whether the students are actually learning anything; it can be hugely dependent on whether the board is clean, the bins have been emptied and how many students you have lost that term.

The quality cycle within the institution, at first glance to me, comprised many aspects that in the interim seemed confusing. There are a number of bureaucratic elements including action plans/reviews that I was required to evaluate not only in terms of my performance as an individual but as they relate to the curriculum team. There is a requirement to evaluate the impact you/your team has made on the learning experience. Although this process could seem just like a form-filling exercise, if evaluated throughout the year this could be a useful process that sparks discussion within the team for best and shared practice. However, I felt that throughout my first years of teaching that colleagues found this process quite tedious and could not see the usefulness of this exercise. I feel that what you fail to realise within your first year of teaching is the impact that these reviews can have, in terms of grades the college is awarded, and the outcomes in terms of funding from the local authority.

One of the elements of quality reviews that I do find the most useful is the student review. Twice a year students are asked to evaluate the teaching provision for each class. There are questions regarding the quality of teaching, quality of the resources and the feedback from homework.

The students are without doubt the most honest consumers, who highlighted the elements that they thought could be improved. I very quickly tried to change and incorporate their suggestions and unsurprisingly they were usually right. Positive comments boosted my confidence to continue with elements that they felt were successful. Without doubt I personally feel that this provides the best judge of the quality of their learning experience within the classroom.

Of course one of the most recognised forms of the assessment of quality within the classroom and the college as a whole is that of the inspection process. The Enhanced

Wider Review and Ofsted visitations are among the most stressful experiences for the new teacher.

You can plan and prepare for the inspection only not to be observed. This can be quite frustrating for you as you somehow feel cheated out of the opportunity to shine.

The process, however, can also be quite stressful for the students within the class. It is my experience that they find it equally nerve-racking and do not like new people in the class. They often feel they have to be respectfully quiet during the class and this can lead to an impression of disengagement to the inspector. No matter how hard you reassure them that the inspection is assessing your performance they still experience an element of uncomfortable infringement in what they perceive as their learning environment.

No matter how hard you try as a new teacher to make sure your quality of teaching is to the highest standard, no matter how much effort you put into your resources for your classroom, how approachable you are in offering pastoral support to your students or how good your results and retention are, at the end of the day, the quality of the provision will still be measured by the learners. This can be largely dependent on whether the students can park their cars, whether the library is too noisy and whether the price of the food is too costly in the canteen.

Observation of teaching and learning

In most organisations each member of staff is observed once during each year. This is normally carried out by a line manager or an advanced practitioner. The quality of teaching input is generally evaluated over a relatively long period, and takes into account the nature of the input, i.e. its appropriateness, the knowledge of learning theory, skills as a lecturer and skills as a facilitator of learning. Observation is an attempt to monitor and guarantee the quality of input into the placement organisation's teaching operations. Quality is all important; it rarely emerges 'accidentally', but is a direct product of an effective teaching–learning partnership.

The evaluation of staff can help to maintain the organisation's professional standards. Most staff understand the necessity of honing their skills and keeping abreast of a rapidly changing educational environment and require feedback that enables them to understand their strengths and areas for development.

In order to encourage consistency of feedback and to provide clear evidence to support grading decisions, standard documentation is used and observations are normally graded using the Ofsted grading criteria shown below.

- Grade 1 – Outstanding.
- Grade 2 – Good.
- Grade 3 – Satisfactory.
- Grade 4 – Unsatisfactory.

It is essential that the process adopted by the organisation is able to provide this quality of experience because staff will want to know to what extent they are meeting the expectations of students and the organisation, and how they can develop their practice.

Quality is inextricably linked with funding. Consistently good quality of teaching and learning will be rewarded by local authorities through the 'provider performance review' process. Satisfactory provision will trigger support in devising improvement strategies. Unsatisfactory provision may ultimately mean sanctions.

Observation is an important part in the continuous improvement of further education providers. In many colleges now any member of staff being grade 3 or 4 in an observation will be required to partake in extra training and then a re-observation. The effect of this on teachers is that it is no longer acceptable for teachers to be 'satisfactory' – they need to achieve 'good' or 'outstanding' in their observations in order to retain employment in the sector. However, we have to have systems that enable them to achieve this standard and to allow them to maximise their potential. This includes observations that are consistent, fair and give them an equal chance to get a high grade.

The observer should be suitably qualified and experienced in conducting observations. They should have undertaken training in current observation procedures and should have carried out joint observations to ensure their competence to observe. Observers should sit somewhere that provides a good view of the teacher and the learner activities. This position may change but they should be unobtrusive at all times. They should be able to look at learners' work and speak to them if a suitable opportunity arises. The observer will observe a section of a lesson not normally longer than one hour and will formulate their grade based on evidence gathered in that time.

Observers are also responsible for ensuring the equality and fairness of the system. It is the responsibility of the organisation to provide equal treatment and opportunities for all staff. The concept of fairness is difficult to describe, but is bound up in issues of equality of opportunity and consistency of standards and judgements.

It is critical that the process is supportive and developmental. The observer will need to decide how to ensure the trainee feels valued throughout the process even though some of the messages may be about improvements needed, or about how to help staff identify different ways of approaching less successful practice and how to reinforce and build on their best practice.

The ultimate purpose of the observation system is to help bring about improvements in the quality of the experience of learners and their achievements. Observers cannot impose change, but can be catalysts in enabling individual members of staff to identify possible changes and ways of bringing them about. Targets for development should be owned by the member of staff, be specific, measurable and achievable, have a direct impact on the experience of the learner and be monitored during the next observation.

CASE STUDY
My experience of, and reflection on, the observation process
In the past I have often felt that staff are not satisfied with the feedback I have given to them after lesson observations. I have often been so concerned with not upsetting them that I may have failed to get across the important developmental points that would have helped them to improve in the future. This has not been helped by the 'kiss kick kiss' approach. There has often been so much 'kiss' that the 'kick' gets lost in the

process. It can also be difficult to carry out observations on and give feedback to staff whom I have never met or worked with.

One experience of this was when I was asked to observe a trainee teacher who works as a police marksman, training the police to use firearms. I had to go to an army base in Altcar and carry out an observation on a firing range. This type of training is completely outside of my experience and by the time I had travelled 65 miles to get there I was very anxious and stressed. The observation was three hours long and very difficult to assess. I gave him a grade 2 (above average delivery) but in reality have no idea if his training was any better than any other person teaching that subject. So it could quite easily have been a grade 3 (satisfactory – average delivery). It was also extremely difficult to give effective feedback and targets for development when I have minimal subject knowledge. I do question the value of the experience to both the trainee teacher and to myself and the fairness of the grading decision made.

It is imperative that the observation process is moderated and standardised. During a recent Ofsted inspection the lead inspector asked the question 'How do we know that a grade 1 given by one line manager has the same value as a grade 1 given by another line manager?' This is a difficult question to answer and to evidence. In most organisations, members of the quality team will carry out a paper-based audit of the observation reports. This involves observers reading the feedback on the reports and agreeing or disagreeing with the grade awarded.

There are some very obvious problems with this system because it means you are basing the judgement on the quality of the written feedback and not the actual lesson observation. It is very difficult to assess the 'buzz' in a lesson and to know if learning has taken place if you are not actually in the lesson.

The positive outcome of this process is that it focuses attention on the way we write the reports to ensure they reflect the actual lesson and to make judgements that support the grade awarded. A paper-based moderation of the paperwork lacks some credibility but does give a baseline assessment of the quality of the report and a 'guide' only to the accuracy of the grading decision.

Staff have the right to fair and accurate grades and there is a need for more standardisation via the use of joint observations to ensure that the observers are as similar as possible in their assessments.

Giving feedback

The structure of the 'reflective discussion' or feedback meeting that should be held between the observer and the observee should be based on research and current practice in other organisations. It is important to be specific, offer a solution, be sensitive and to give the feedback face to face. This is often an area that is overlooked or paid lip-service to. Feedback can often be formulaic and very general, leaving staff with little to go on in order to improve in the future. Traditional approaches have included the feedback sandwich, giving praise, areas for improvement and then praise again. However, this technique is not widely supported. Research suggests that we remember the first thing and last thing we are told, and not much in between, which means that by using the feedback sandwich technique teachers may not remember the areas for improvement and so not be able to improve their practice.

When discussing feedback in relation to teacher observations it may be necessary to choose carefully the content and the order of our feedback and to think about using clear targets for development to allow staff to continue to develop their practice and to improve their teaching skills over time.

By using hierarchical feedback we mean that there is a limit to how much feedback a teacher can absorb and this is often in the region of only three or four points. It is important to cover the most important point first, then the second most important point and so on. If the threshold of understanding is reached by the fourth point, it is less of a problem.

Internal inspection

Most organisations in the sector will have systems of internal inspection. These are often 'mini' Ofsted inspections carried out by a senior management team or external consultants. The process often involves a full audit of a department over a period of a week or two. This normally includes the following elements.

- Observation of all teachers.
- Auditing of teaching files and evidence files.
- Meetings with staff and students.
- Feedback from students.
- Consideration of data and results.

This process will normally culminate in a report and an action plan for that department, which is monitored and tracked. This report normally includes an overall grade based on the Ofsted criteria and will mirror that which Ofsted might have given if they had carried out the same inspection at the same time.

Departments are normally given a period of notice for the inspection and these inspections often follow a biannual rolling programme. However, some organisations choose to focus on areas that are underperforming and leave those deemed to be outstanding uninspected for some period of time.

Staff tend to take these internal inspections very seriously and prepare extensively for them. This is often a good time to update resources and tidy classrooms. Most staff feel ownership of the resulting report and action plan because they have been deeply involved in the process and, providing the feedback is fair and justified, can identify how to improve things in the future.

PRACTICAL TASK PRACTICAL TASK PRACTICAL TASK PRACTICAL TASK PRACTICAL TASK

Investigate the system of internal inspection in your organisation and see if you can read the last report written about your department.
- Does it seem fair and accurate?
- Is the action plan being monitored?

Self-assessment

Self-assessment is a powerful tool. Undertaken rigorously on the basis of evidence, it can help colleges to identify the strengths they can celebrate and the weaknesses they need to address. Followed up by action-planning, systematically monitored implementation and the setting of challenging but achievable targets, self-assessment can help achieve real, measurable improvements.

Its other benefits include:

- a potential to involve all staff in a genuine culture of continuous improvement;
- the evidence it gives of a growing maturity in the sector;
- the ability to take responsibility for the quality of its own provision;
- the corresponding opportunity to be subject to a 'lighter touch' in external assessments.

Colleges are becoming far more sophisticated and skilled in making judgements about their performance on the basis of evidence and using those judgements to identify and plan for action for further improvement. At the same time, the quality and range of information available to colleges relating to their own performance, and that of others, has also improved, so that judgements are easier to make. In many colleges a self-critical, improving culture has been created, in which most staff value the role of regular, rigorous annual self-assessment in helping them improve further. Self-assessment has been integrated into current practice and in many colleges it is now an integral part of the college annual review and planning cycles.

All providers of education in the lifelong learning sector have to produce a self-assessment report in a set format every year and submit it to the government via the local authority. This self-assessment report is used by Ofsted as the basis of its inspection planning process. The key questions Ofsted will ask when it inspects a college are:

- does the self-assessment report show a true and valid picture of the organisation?
- can it have confidence in the organisation's ability to assess its own performance?

If Ofsted is satisfied, then it will be more likely to give higher grades to the organisation, particularly for leadership and management.

The questions colleges need to ask themselves are:

How well are we doing?
Once data is collected about current performance, it is possible to make a judgement about the quality of performance, especially if benchmarking data are also available so that a college can compare its performance with that of other colleges. These judgements can either be made internally as part of an annual self-assessment process, or externally in an inspection. In colleges, these judgements are usually expressed as key strengths and weaknesses.

What do we need to do to improve?
Identifying key strengths and weaknesses makes it relatively easy to identify areas that need improvement and benchmarking data can help indicate the extent of the improvement

needed, which can in turn inform the target set. How does this fit with overall plans/direction of the college?

It is important that areas for improvement are integrated into annual operational plans and that they are consistent with, and help inform, the overall strategic direction of the college. It is then also important to draw up detailed plans specifying action to be taken, who is responsible, the target for improvement, the timescale and the arrangements for monitoring progress and evaluating success.

Are improvements taking place?

Once plans are in place, their implementation needs to be systematically monitored and decisions made about their effectiveness. Once targets are achieved, the college may wish to set its quality standards slightly higher as it starts to go round the quality improvement cycle for the second time.

REFLECTIVE TASK

Ask your line manager if you can see the self-assessment report for your department. Reflect on the report and how you can contribute to the action plan for improvement.

Self-regulation

Self-regulation includes self-assessment but is a wider concept. It offers a vision of a FE sector as a respected, autonomous, demand-led organisation. It will act both individually and collectively within a self-regulation system; deliver high quality, responsive provision for the benefit of learners, employers, communities and the nation; and operate as a respected and trusted partner of government.

Colleges and organisations are being encouraged to form clusters and to carry out self-regulating activities amongst themselves. They will achieve this by working collaboratively to raise the quality of tier provision, which may ultimately lead to less formal 'external' inspection and more trust in organisations to regulate themselves.

The Single Voice for Self Regulation represents the sector in strategic dialogue with government on regulatory matters. It represents and supports providers in interpreting and responding to regulatory directives set by government and national agencies.

In doing so, it accepts and recognises the distinctive voices of representative bodies from different parts of the sector. It is responsible for developing, implementing and maintaining the framework for self-regulation and developing a rolling programme of activity for this purpose.

As this book goes to print this is a relatively new development in the sector and, although some pilot projects have taken place, it is not yet clear how this will embed itself into the sector.

Find out if your organisation has taken part in any self-regulation projects. If so, what is the outcome?

CASE STUDY
George Woodall, curriculum leader

Having worked in FE for only 18 months, and having been recently appointed as curriculum leader of Carpentry and Joinery, the prospect of being in charge of the implementation of a standardised quality-improvement plan for the department was quite daunting.

Although over the last academic year the behaviour, retention and achievement of learners were on the increase, some courses still presented a cause for concern, and feedback to and from learners was non-existent.

Growth was not in line with college demands and within the department there was not a standard approach regarding the quality of provision. I had to develop a strategy of getting the department on board. Some of the lecturers had over 20 years' experience and could be adverse to a radical change to the processes, procedures and approach within the department and how we as a department would move forward. I considered this was to be my major challenge.

The strategy that I adopted was that of team work – getting the lecturers and technicians working together to overcome the culture of 'that will do' from past years. We, as a department, decided what had to change and how to change it, representing a collaborative redesign of the department.

Individuals were tasked to redesign the schemes of work and practical assessment plans ready for the introduction of the new curriculum. The enthusiasm demonstrated by the members of staff working together and building on each others' ideas was inspiring and this new-found ethos of working together culminated in developing high quality lessons and sharing within the department.

We were reinventing the wheel to meet the needs of the awarding body, the college's internal quality department and our own self-pride. I realised that I had to bring all the changes together, and with this in mind I designed an online tracking system which would link the internal verification process to the progress tracking of the individual learner. With this tracking system open to all, we had made the department transparent and this provided a sense of pride in showing what we can do as a department when we work together.

The outcome of the changes made within the department was that of self-belief in that we could work together in developing and sharing best practice and this showed in the figures for achievement and retention 2008–09. All statistics showed that we were above the national average and the results were the best in several years. Having worked with the newly introduced quality systems for a year, we diagnosed where they were imperfect, and planned to further develop them over the summer recess aiming for implementation in September 2009. It was expected to build on the previous success.

Having had such misgivings at the beginning of the quality process, I now consider myself fortunate that I had a nucleus of lecturers who had the vision of raising the profile of the department within the college. Full circle feedback provided the most benefit as the learners provided feedback to the lecturer of what they considered was good and what could be improved upon. This, together with the lecturers actually listening to the learners, ensured that the improvements made so far to the quality of provision have been significant. We still have a long way to go before we are truly outstanding. However, the initial steps have been taken and the change in culture now means that we are increasingly likely to get there.

As we can see from this case study, the main influence on the ability for departments to improve is the willingness of staff to engage with the process and to share good practice and resources amongst themselves.

A SUMMARY OF **KEY POINTS**

In this chapter we have:

> **explored themes of self-regulation, self-assessment and internal inspection in education;**

> **discussed the role of observation in raising standards;**

> **considered the role of staff in engaging with the quality agenda;**

> **identified strategies that will enable you to understand the systems in place in your organisation.**

REFERENCES REFERENCES REFERENCES REFERENCES REFERENCES REFERENCES

Heider, J (1985) *The Tao of Leadership*. Atlanta, GA: Humanics.

FURTHER READING FURTHER READING FURTHER READING FURTHER READING

You might like to read the following books:

Steward, A (2009) *Continuing your Professional Development in Lifelong Learning*. London: Continuum.
This book focuses on developing your professional role within the organisation. It provides an interesting insight into the role of CPD in creating professional staff.

Fairclough, M (2008) *Supporting Learners in the Lifelong Learning Sector*. Maidenhead: Open University Press.
This book is good because it focuses on the specific issues around supporting learners and how we as teachers can deal with their complex needs.

Also:

Goleman, D (2005) *Emotional Intelligence*. London: Bantam Books.

MacBeath, J and McGlynn, A (2002) *Self Evaluation – What's In It For Schools?* London: RoutledgeFalmer.

Montgomery, D (2002) *Helping Teachers Develop Through Classroom Observation.* London: David Fulton Publishing.

Websites

Department for Business Innovation and Skills www.bis.gov
Single Voice for Self Regulation www.feselfregulation.org.uk

5
Assessment: moderation and verification

This chapter is designed to:

- provide you with a clear understanding of the quality assurance issues that are associated with assessment;
- recognise the public and political arena in which the outcomes from assessment will be debated;
- identify the necessary procedures to be followed to ensure that learners are assessed in the right way and achieve at the right level;
- outline some of the essential administrative processes in which you may be involved;
- highlight the impact – for both learners and institution – if essential administrative processes are not addressed correctly.

It addresses the following Professional Standards for QTLS:

AS 5 Collaboration with other individuals, groups and/or organisations with a legitimate interest in the progress and development of learners.

AK 5.1 Ways to communicate and collaborate with colleagues and/or others to enhance learners' experience.

ES 5 Working within the systems and quality requirements of the organisation in relation to assessment and monitoring of learner progress.

EK 5.1 The role of assessment and associated organisational procedures in relation to the quality cycle.

EK 5.2 The assessment requirements of individual learning programmes and procedures for conducting and recording internal and/or external assessments.

EK 5.3 The necessary/appropriate assessment information to communicate to others who have a legitimate interest in learner achievement.

Introduction: what is assessment for?

REFLECTIVE TASK

Write down what you think is the fundamental purpose of assessment.

There are arguably two historic approaches to assessment that have been evident in British education in the last 30 years: assessment *of* learning and assessment *for* learning. To some extent they can divide teachers into two camps.

A simplistic approach is to equate assessment *of* learning with a process that determines whether or not a learner is good enough to receive their qualification. It is reflected in the test and exam mentality, the banner headlines of popular papers with the appeal that dumbing down is prevalent and that school and college leavers are not as intelligent as their predecessors. It is an approach that wants assessment to be tough and robust and to sort out the sheep and the goats, the wheat and the chaff.

The other approach is to recognise that learning is a complex and challenging process and that one size rarely fits all. It sees the process of assessment as an interaction with learners, a dialogue where learning can be owned and that the outcome is for fair and appropriate progress towards a meaningful and relevant goal. This is assessment *for* learning.

Where does your answer to the reflective task place you?

Assessment as a political hot potato

Your orientation towards assessment will be important because it may arguably colour your approach towards two of the most important quality assurance processes related to assessment within the sector, namely moderation and verification, which we will consider shortly.

However, you must also recognise that – whichever inclination your answer showed – assessment has become a very politicised process, with an incremental rise in importance every year since the introduction of school and college league tables. You are probably familiar with the annual headlines in the press that accompany A level and GCSE results and the subsequent publication of the league tables where the very public availability of learner achievements sparks all sorts of argument in the staffroom, board room and living room. The fact that the BBC has a webpage – http://news.bbc.co.uk/1/hi/education/league_tables – devoted to school and college league tables serves as an indicator of how prevalent a target-driven approach to education has become and how easily the quality debate can become simplified into a performance mentality. We will consider this in more detail later.

Casualties of assessment

The public nature of the evidence and the debate over assessment has had some high-profile casualties along the way. August 2002 saw the results published for the newly revised A level curriculum that introduced AS and A2 papers. Such was the public and political furore over the suitability and reliability of the exams, the results that they generated and the accusations of political interference, that by October of that year the two major protagonists, Sir William Stubbs, Chair of the QCA, and Estelle Morris, Secretary of State for Education, had both resigned. This was despite the fact that the Tomlinson Report, commissioned to investigate into the situation, broadly found each free of blame (Tomlinson, 2004). Richardson (2007) looks at this event, and other episodes, with a view to consider how some problems become unmanageable, while others can be successfully addressed, and what is clear is that education and politics are indeed a volatile mix.

A further example can be seen more recently when, in 2008, QCA cancelled with immediate effect its five-year national curriculum tests contract with ETS Europe, a contract worth £156 million. This followed the fiasco around marking of the tests that saw papers not delivered, wrongly delivered, not marked at all, and so on, all of which delayed publication of results with serious questions about the reliability of the scores. This robust action in cancelling the contract, and a payment by ETS of £19.5 million payment to the QCA, did not prevent QCA Chair, Ken Boston, having to resign over the event and the damning report that accompanied it.

One significant development, specifically coming from the problems that QCA have faced, was the creation of the Office of Qualifications and Examinations Regulation (Ofqual) to have a specific focus on ensuring, in their own words, that *all learners get the results they deserve and that their qualifications are correctly valued and understood, now and in the future* (Ofqual, 2010) This is a website worth visiting and being very familiar with: www.ofqual.gov.uk.

Teachers' reactions to assessment

Others in the sector are engaging with the issues regarding assessment outcomes and league tables from a very different point of view. In the staffroom, the teaching unions are protesting against what they see as inappropriate assessment. The campaign against the national tests (sometimes know as SATs) has been growing in voice – *Teachers' union votes to boycott SATs* (*Guardian*, 2009) – and culminated in the first actual action in 2010, with reports of a quarter of primary schools boycotting the tests (BBC, 2010). Working in a different direction, teachers and their unions have been looking to advocate a focus on the achievement of learners and the efforts of their teachers, sustaining a debate about the complex and challenging nature of the work and seeking to enhance the reputation of the profession. In a recent speech, Dr Mary Bousted, General Secretary of the Association of Teachers and Lecturers, said:

> *It's quite simple and very complex all at the same time. It's the question, what makes the difference to learners' achievements? Now you all know what research tells us, but politicians have conveniently ignored in recent years, that the most difference comes from learners' social and family backgrounds. But setting that aside, what makes the most difference within our schools and colleges?*
>
> *It's the teachers, stupid.*
>
> *While clever policy wonks spent years looking for some other holy grail of shortcuts to raising achievement, you carried on proving in your classrooms that there are no shortcuts.*
>
> *What I mean is that teachers undertake the most complex, challenging and creative work and that the professional knowledge and skill that they possess has not been sufficiently acknowledged or supported by politicians, by the press or by society at large.*
>
> (Bousted, 2010)

Admirable rhetoric, and not without some commendation, but regardless of how good or otherwise teachers may be (and in passing it is worth noting that the National Teaching Awards do not have a category for anyone working in the post-compulsory sector), there remain constant complaints from other stakeholders.

Employers' views

Take the regular denunciations from the employers in the form of the Confederation of British Industry (CBI), which has an enviable track record of saying school leavers are never good enough to do the job (whatever job they have in mind). A quick trawl of archived documents found newspaper and televisions accounts for 2004, 2006, 2009 and 2010 detailing the dissatisfaction, although my own memory takes me back to the 1980s when employers were chanting the same mantra. A recent example would be *The Times'* reporting of the comments of Sir Stuart Rose, executive chairman of Marks & Spencer at the CBI conference in November 2009: *We have to worry about those people who don't have the 21st-century equivalent of metal-bashing, whether that is computer literacy or something. They are not fit for work when they come out of college.* He echoed comments made in the previous month by Sir Terry Leahy, the chief executive of Tesco, in saying that too many school leavers could not read, write or do arithmetic (*The Times,* 2010).

Such public recitation of dissatisfaction is a source of endless embarrassment for whichever government, of whatever political persuasion, is in control of our education system and particularly its assessment outcomes. Since most children spend at least 12 years in compulsory education and, given it is an area of national investment not entirely devoid of resources and research, these sorts of complaints – admittedly simplified in both origin and in reporting – remain embarrassing.

What we have been looking at here are aspects of the tension within both the compulsory and post-compulsory sectors of education when faced with the question 'what is quality education?' How do we define and measure success in education? Is it by the outcomes of 'assessment *of*' or 'assessment *for*'? Where you want to invest your energy will, as we have suggested, be informed by your initial disposition towards assessment. But do note: while there are challenges and criticism regarding the *how* and *what* of assessment, there is every likelihood that at some point in your career you will be asked directly to account for the success or otherwise of your learners. At this point, it will be useful to explore the requirements of two key components of the assessment process as you may experience them. But first, a story …

CASE STUDY
The tale of the locked filing cabinet
A colleague had been given some basic literacy to teach as part of an introductory construction course. Before the Moser Report (1999), there was not always best practice in addressing the needs of those students requiring support with adult basic skills and it was not uncommon just to timetable staff on such a course because they were down on teaching hours, rather than they were actually the best person to do the work. (So, you will notice, there is the first weakness in the quality chain.)

Towards the end of the course the External Moderator was coming in to assess the work. To be blunt, my colleague had not been on top of the course requirements. There had been lessons, the students had done exercises, learning had taken place but he had not, somewhat unfortunately, got the students to undertake the formal assignments that were required.

Faced with the disturbing news that the External Moderator wanted to sample the basic literacy work, he had to fall back on subterfuge and claimed the work was locked in his filing cabinet and that he had left the key at home. At the insistence of the External Moderator and direction from his manager he was sent home to retrieve the key.

Now, as with most tales, they grow in the telling and when this was related to me the purported outcome was that he actually never came back!

While it is clear that the person concerned was clearly negligent (even before the advent of professional standards and the Code of Conduct, see Chapter 8), there are some pertinent questions to ask.

Knowing that he was not a trained teacher of literacy, why was he asked to do the work? What support was he given? Who was responsible for the overall assessment of the programme and for making sure everything was ready for external scrutiny? Where was the process of internal moderation, which would have shone a light on the impending problem in advance of the external visit? To what extent was there a culture of individual and collaborative responsibility? While not condoning the poor practice that is so clearly evident, these are all questions to address.

The process and practice of moderation and verification

You may not be involved in both processes – it will very much depend on your curriculum – but you should be aware of them and capable of engaging with them in the most effective and appropriate way.

Moderation

Found where there is a partial or whole coursework element, moderation can be described simply as the process of adjusting an assessment decision – a mark or grade – so that it is in line with national standards and provides a fair and accurate reflection of a learner's performance. There are two elements, internal moderation and external moderation.

Internal moderation will require a sampling of completed work by members of the teaching team and a reassessment against provided exemplars. It may be that someone has attended a training event to take a Lead Moderator role or that exemplars have been provided directly with commentary on how to apply the mark/grading scheme in each case. The goal is for an honest and consistent application of the requisite criteria and the adjustment of marks if necessary.

In terms of quality assurance there is an implicit contract between teachers, learners and award bodies that marks or grades will be awarded fairly and will be a direct assessment of the actual performance. However, given that any one teacher or course team may not interpret and apply the mark/grade scheme in a reliable way, it is necessary to have another line of moderation.

External moderation is an additional level of sampling and re-marking carried out by a designated person external to your organisation. An External Moderator may come to the college or you may be required to send a sample to them. (This often depends on the curriculum and specific subject – you can't really put car engines in the post!) Either way, they provide a necessary level of independent scrutiny.

In terms of your role and responsibility there are some simple, fundamental requirements that you need to address. Regardless of how new or inexperienced you are, you will need to know what to do to ensure that work is assessed appropriately and in good time.

- Ask the course leader if there is any course work to be formally assessed within the programme and, if the answer is 'yes', ask for specific details regarding its format and assessment strategy and enquire about examples from previous years that may have been kept as a standard or a benchmark.

- Secure accurate and current information about deadlines. If you are obliged to work with a course leader who says things like, 'well it's usually the third or fourth week in March', confidently take responsibility and check for yourself on the (correct) award body website. The award bodies are hugely keen to get work in on time and so signpost key dates very clearly. They will also have advice on guidance on how to comply with course work requirements.
- Work out when you are going to require work to be submitted from your students to meet any internal and external moderation deadlines. When I started marking GCSE psychology, you were allowed to select a range of coursework across top/middle/bottom performance and send this off to your External Moderator. More recently, there has been a change in practice whereby the External Moderator, on behalf of the award body, chooses the sample of candidates' work. This means that you must have all of your candidates' work ready at the appointed date.

If the External Moderator approves your sample, the marks you have given to the remaining candidates are confirmed. If you are consistently high or low no further sample would necessarily be required but an adjustment will be applied across all your candidates using a statistical formula. If your marking is erratic a further sample might be required to establish the best adjustment or, in extreme cases, all the work will be called in and re-marked by the External Moderator.

TOP TIPS TOP TIPS **TOP TIPS** TOP TIPS **TOP TIPS** TOP TIPS **TOP TIPS** TOP TIPS

It is often advisable to tell your students that marks/grades are only ever provisional until external confirmation has been received: it is not great to tell your student they have got an A in their coursework and then it comes back from the exam board as a C.

Verification

Verification is different to moderation in that it is focuses on confirmation that the right process has been followed in order to demonstrate that the candidate has been successful in achieving the competences, standards, criteria that create the qualification. More commonly found within the NVQ curriculum and other vocational awards, it is a method of quality assuring the organisation of assessment evidence and to demonstrate that it complies with the specific themes of currency, sufficiency and relevancy. It is worth noting that with some awards, verification will include some moderation of marking also.

In terms of your responsibility, one essential aspect of verification is compliance with the published process in organising the evidence that shows the candidate has achieved the award. You will be looking to ensure that your learners have provided the required range of evidence, at the right level and in the appropriate format. If you are not sure, speak to your team leader and other colleagues. Internal verification will be an ongoing process with deadlines decided by the team or possibly co-ordinated across a department.

The Internal Verifier will scrutinise your learners' portfolio of evidence in anticipation of any external verification. You need to understand the approach that External Verifiers (EV) will adopt and that your Internal Verifier will expect to be addressed. An EV will not necessarily be re-marking in the way a moderator might: they are looking to confirm decisions by scrutinising evidence and agreeing it is current, sufficient and relevant. They want straightforward and effective access to a range of work from different candidates and different assessors.

As a Head of Department, I was advised that most verifiers operated by a 'two minute' rule of thumb. Having decided, or been directed to, which elements and which evidence were to be the focus of the visit, if a verifier could not find the evidence they were looking for within two minutes they would assume it wasn't there. And, if it wasn't there, the portfolio was incomplete and therefore the award could not be claimed.

Such is the thoroughness that has been sought over the evolution of vocational awards over time that there are specific professional qualifications for the roles of Assessor and Verifier (often referred to as the A Awards and V Awards) that are a requirement for staff working in this curriculum area.

Direct Claim Status

Effective and successful internal and external verification are valuable elements of a successful internal and external inspection (see Chapters 3 and 4) because they provide a short cut to an important quality measure that Ofsted and QAA might consider. Because of the investment necessary in external verification, in terms of the human resource of actual verifiers, award bodies became keen to facilitate independence of centres if they were able to demonstrate a consistent and reliable approach to the quality assurance of the process. This independence is known as Direct Claim Status (DCS).

There is a significant benefit for centres also, because if they achieve DCS they can claim certification – and therefore successful completion – sooner rather than later, as they would not have to wait for the next scheduled visit by the External Verifier. In other words, if you can prove you can verify the assessment process to the highest standards you are trusted to undertake it with minimal supervision, which, in turn, can: reduce the anxiety of an External Verifier's visit; reduce the frequency of visits; and facilitate more frequent and quicker claims. What's not to like? The achievement of DCS is both a kitemark of satisfaction and a boon to supporting the quality assurance of the assessment process within a department or a centre's Self-Assessment Report (SAR) when Ofsted comes to call.

The award bodies have stated criteria for the achievement of DCS and this will be something your Exams Officer or Lead Internal Verifier will be responsible for. You do have a part to play, however, because the criteria expect all members of a course to comply with the requirements. It will depend on the reports completed by an External Moderator/Verifier when they visit and will require achievement of minimum levels of quality and satisfactory compliance with any previous actions plans, usually over a timescale of at least two visits. So, don't be the one letting the side down.

Centre Risk Assessment

Parallel to this positive award of independence, quality management strategies have encouraged the development of tools such as the Edexcel Centre Risk Assessment (CRA) Policy with regard to BTEC awards.

Their stated policy is as follows:

> We aim to reduce the bureaucratic burden of assessment and assessment-related processes on centres whilst maintaining the quality of provision. We will achieve

this through effecting a change of focus from an Edexcel-driven model of 'Quality Control' to one of centre-driven 'Quality Assurance'.

(BTEC mission statement, Edexcel, 2010)

Both approaches, those of DCS and CRA, are robust in seeking to quality assure the assessment process of a provider, and both allow for sanctions if standards are not good enough. There is a sliding scale of remedial action required until such a point at which the award body will no longer approve qualifications claimed by a centre. Given that funding is explicitly tied to successful completion (see later section on success rates), then there are serious financial implications for any organisation that finds itself in this position. It will be paying for the cost of delivering teaching – staffing, resources – and the cost of registration with the award body, but will be unable to claim funding where this is tied to outcomes which are held in abeyance until satisfactory standards of assessment can once again be demonstrated.

Reflection on these detailed processes of moderation and verification will confirm just how far a commitment to quality improvement has moved us on from the original story in the case study above.

Your involvement in the QA and QI of assessment

Throughout this book we are trying to strike a balance between signposting you to the 'non-teaching' responsibilities within the job that are both expected and – if executed correctly – very valuable, and creating an overwhelming sense of there being too much paperwork to do. So let's consider two sides of the challenge, something we could call *input* and *output*.

CASE STUDY

GCSE English literature – 'What are we reading this year, sir?'

Read the following edited account from the BBC News website.

Pupils at a private school went into an English Literature GCSE exam having been taught the wrong book.

Fifth-formers at the boys' school had been expecting to answer questions on John Steinbeck's Of Mice and Men. *The exam board, OCR, said the text had been on the approved list but had been replaced in January and that the school had been notified twice.*

The students should have been taught one of Things Fall Apart, *by Chinua Achebe,* The Old Man and the Sea, *by Ernest Hemingway, or George Orwell's* 1984.

Twenty-four pupils at the school were affected by the error, although the school said of the two questions listed, the students could answer both. 'We have to hold our hands up here and say it's our fault and we will do all we can,' said deputy headmaster.

'We contacted the parents of the affected students ourselves to explain the problem. We have begun an internal investigation to ensure this does not happen again. The exam boards are used to this happening. It is not unusual to find pupils studied the wrong text.'

A spokeswoman for Oxford, Cambridge and RSA (OCR) said pupils' marks were not affected by their teachers' mistake. 'It's one of those things that's not really our fault in this case,' she added. 'The school has made an error on their part. We've done all we can to communicate with the school, they've had at least two notices this year.'

BBC News (2010)

Well, would you want to be the teacher knocking on the principal's door to admit this gaff? Or to be facing irate students and angry parents?

REFLECTIVE TASK

Having read the article above, make a note of what you think has gone wrong and how it could be avoided in the future. (And please note, it's not an isolated example.)

Hopefully you would have considered the responsibility of the individual teacher to make use of the readily available information from the award body and ensure they were up to date. But there would also be the possibility that someone senior should have monitored the progress of all the staff by scrutinising their basic schemes of work for the year. Or maybe there needs to be a development of a shared and supportive team culture: a simple team meeting to discuss this year's texts might have done the trick. This is the *input* side of assessment, something that requires your fullest attention.

Exams are such a high-profile feature of education that mistakes can be costly in terms of reputation, but the whole assessment process is also stringently tied to funding so that any shortfall in success will eventually translate into financial costs to the organisation. We"ll revisit this in Chapter 10 but we now need to look at some important *output* measures that are central to an appreciation of the quality assurance of assessment.

Outcomes from assessment

Success rates

In the introductory chapter we advised you that you will have to become used to using data. One of the most fundamental sets of data is that of success rates. Success rates are used as a principal measure in reviewing the quality of delivery for qualifications and cohorts of learners. In management terms, improvement in success rates is the key indicator of quality improvement.

You have a responsibility to be aware of three essential measures of the data and how they are used to provide the success rates created by teaching, learning and assessment.

1. *Retention* is a measure of not dropping out.
It is calculated by dividing the number of learners in a cohort or group completing a programme by the number of starters.

2. *Achievement* is a measure of outcomes for those who complete the course.
It is calculated by dividing the number of learners achieving a qualification by the number who finish the course.

3. *Success* is a measure of outcomes based on how many actually started the course.
It is calculated by dividing the number of learners achieving a qualification by the number who started the course.

Example

We take a cohort of 25 learners who started a BTEC National Diploma in Public Services – 5 leave before the end of the programme so 20 finish.

Retention rate: finishers/starters $\times$ 100, or $20/25 \times 100 = 80\%$

The retention rate is 80%.

If 2 learners of the 20 who finished were not actually successful then we have:

Achievement rate: achievers/finishers $\times$ 100, or $18/20 \times 100 = 90\%$

The achievement rate is 90%.

For this cohort, the success rate would be a measure of those who finished and were successful out of the original of 25 who started.

Success rate: achievers/starts $\times$ 100, or $18/25 \times 100 = 72\%$

The success rate is 72%.

The success rate is a more demanding figure than the achievement rate because it lays a responsibility on the organisation to retain as many learners as possible and to ensure they achieve an outcome.

Now, what we don't know is if a 72% success rate is any good. It might not seem so but we really don't know. This is where data tables for success rates are useful and where a proactive approach on your part is vital.

Benchmarking using success rates

Success rates are a key measure in the Effectiveness dimension of the FfE, which is, at present, central to the quality and funding relationship between colleges and work-based learning providers and the SFA. The LSC in its final year before handing over to the SFA produced Minimum Levels of Performance Reports (MLPs), which examine provider performance against minimum success rate targets for different types of provision. In 2009–10 these were as follows:

- 50% FE long.
- 60% FE short.
- 85% FE very short.
- 40% for WBL Frameworks.

These are for the overall minimum levels of success rate for a provider in terms of any of these types of qualifications. But they can also be used to benchmark your own performance at a subject specific level. Another way to get a measure of the quality of your own teaching and learning is to make use of published tables that are available for specific subjects, say A level psychology or GCSE English (just use a search engine, e.g. 'A level psychology pass rates').

This is not an uncritical focus on data tables: the fact is that, whether you like it or not, someone, internally or externally, is going to compare and contrast the outcomes of your learners – and by implication the quality of your teaching – with the national picture. So you may as well be proactive in having a basic understanding of how and where these figures come from and how you will be judged by them. Knowing how well you are doing and being able to account for it, be it a positive picture or a negative one, is valuable at any stage of your career.

Other QA and QI elements of assessment: Value Added and Distance Travelled

You also need to be aware of the concepts of 'Value Added' (VA) and 'Distance Travelled' (DT). Following much criticism of the lack of context in the crude 'league table of results' approach, government departments now make use of the concept of value added in recognising that every learner is starting from a different point in terms of locality, family, prior achievement, and so on. To this end, based on their achievements at GCSE, a learner achieving a grade C at A level might be considered to have done better than one achieving a grade B. The first may have exceeded expectations, may have 'added value' to their performance, while the other may have stood still in academic terms. A basic differentiation between the terms is that VA applies to graded Level 3 qualifications, most obviously the relationships between GCSE and A level, while DT is a measure applied to outcomes at Levels 1, 2 and 3 and can included non-graded awards, i.e. Pass/Fail.

Your organisation will make use of VA/DT data in different ways, much of it at a senior management level in reporting to YPLA and SFA. For the individual teacher, you will find in many colleges that VA/DT are used with initial assessment to set individual targets for each learner. The acronyms vary – MAG (Minimum Acceptable Grades), MTG (Minimum Target Grades), ITG (Individual Target Grades) – but all are being used to sustain a more personalised approach to learning, to be a focus within the personal tutorial and review system. Again, it may seem like more work but you are unlikely to be asked to do the value added calculations yourself. Rather, it is a sense of commitment to your learners, to knowing about them and working with them, and the most appropriate way of evaluating their actual results. This is an important concept to understand and a commendable strategy to adopt and apply in your own work with your learners.

A final thought

Whether we are advocates of 'assessment for learning' or 'assessment of learning', it should be clear that assessment is an area that does need to be quality assured. For better or worse it is the standard by which most learners, parents, employers and governments judge their teachers. Such is the weight given to the outcomes of assessment, both publicly and privately, that you must make sure that, whatever the debate over the philosophy driving assessment, there is nothing wrong in the processes and practice of its execution, particularly with regard to your personal responsibilities.

A SUMMARY OF **KEY POINTS**

In this chapter we have:

> **considered the key purpose of assessment;**

> **recognised that the outcomes of assessment are under significant popular scrutiny from professionals, politicians and the public;**

> **identified the policy and procedures involved in effective moderation and verification;**

> **identified benefits for learners, teachers and organisations in having strong quality assurance of assessment;**

> **highlighted the importance of success rates and your need to understand them and use them to inform your evaluation and development;**

> **noted the concepts of Value Added and Distance Travelled and emphasised the need to be aware of such measures as they relate to your learners.**

REFERENCES REFERENCES REFERENCES REFERENCES REFERENCES REFERENCES

Bousted, M (2010) *ATL Conference Speech*. www.atl.org.uk/policy-and-campaigns/conference/2010/bousted-conference-2010.asp

EdExcel (2010) *BTEC Centre Risk Assessment 2009–2010 Quick Reference Guide.* London: EdExcel.

Richardson, W (2007) Public Policy Failure and Fiasco in Education: Perspectives on the British Examinations Crises of 2000–2002 and Other Episodes Since 1975. *Oxford Review of Education*, 33 (2):143–60.

The Times (2010) *School Leavers are not up to the job.* http://business.timesonline.co.uk/tol/business/management/article6928861.ece

Tomlinson, M (2002*) Inquiry Into A Level Standards.* London: DFES.

Websites

AQA www.aqa.org.uk

City and Guilds www.cityandguilds.com

Chartered Institute of Educational Assessors www.ciea.org.uk

Data Service www.thedataservice.org.uk

EdExcel www.edexcel.org.uk

Institute for Learning www.ifl.org.uk

Learning and Skills Network www.lsnlearning.org.uk

NEFC www.nefc.org.uk

OCR www.ocr.org.uk

Ofsted www.ofsted.gov.uk

Ofqual www.ofqual.gov.uk

Skills Funding Agency www.skillsfundingagency.com

Teacher Net www.teachernet.gov.uk

The Teaching Awards www.teachingawards.com

6

Listening to learners and evaluating the learners' experience

This chapter is designed to:

- provide you with a clear understanding of the concept of the learner voice;
- recognise the key indicators of quality assurance in terms of listening to learners;
- support you in identifying those polices and procedures that engage with and capture student opinion;
- give you confidence in interpreting feedback from learners;
- seek to establish the concept of ownership and encourage you to be focused on your response.

It addresses the following Professional Standards for QTLS:

AS 4 Reflection and evaluation of their own practice and their continuing professional development as teachers.

AK 4.1 Principles, frameworks and theories which underpin good practice in learning and teaching.

AK 4.2 The impact of own practice on individuals and their learning.

AK 4.3 Ways to reflect, evaluate and use research to develop own practice, and to share good practice with others.

AK 7.1 Organisational systems and processes for recording learner information.

AK 7.2 Own role in the quality cycle.

AK 7.3 Ways to implement improvements based on feedback received.

DS 3 Evaluation of own effectiveness in planning learning.

DK 2.1 The importance of including learners in the planning process.

Introduction

Lies, damned lies and statistics.

(Mark Twain)

This chapter will cover the importance of evaluation and listening to the views of learners, colleagues and other stakeholders in the sector. There will be a focus on the current importance attached to processes of capturing the learner voice, as well as scrutiny of some of the tools at your disposal with which to do this. We will consider the concept of 'ownership' with regard to the outcomes of any evaluation, particularly with a view to examining the debate over establishing QI based on participant feedback, drawing on the old Latin adage, *'Cui bono?'*, in other words 'for whose benefit?'.

REFLECTIVE TASK
REFLECTIVE TASK

Think of the occasions when you have been asked for your opinion as a student.

● How did you engage with the exercise?

● Were you sceptical? Enthusiastic? Indifferent?

● Were you bursting with ideas about how to make a good course better?

● Or did you just have a long list of complaints?

More importantly, did you think it would make any difference? Did you believe that your teachers or your college/university *really* wanted your opinion or did you feel it was some sort of PR exercise that wouldn't have a tangible impact?

Now, I must declare my hand here. As a child of parents who survived the Second World War and who struggled to raise their children in the austerity of the 1950s, which for many continued on into the 1960s, I was raised on the mantra of 'put up and shut up': no, life wasn't fair, not everything was wonderful, some toys did break the first time you used them, you can't have another ice cream and that's life. There wasn't an expectation that things could be better, it was just the way they were.

Contrast that with what can only be called the quality – or some would say 'complaints' – industry that surrounds us today and we can be nothing but astounded by the turn round of events. Changes in legislation and the concomitant growth in publicly funded bodies committed to protecting our interests (OfCOM, OfWAT, OfGEM, etc.), proliferation of litigation-driven solicitors, changes in societal attitudes given the unrestrained mouthpiece of modern media: all have driven a shift in perspective in terms of what we the 'consumer' consider to be appropriate levels of product and service.

So, do we have 'customers', 'clients' or 'consumers' in education? And where might we find them being evident?

Framework for Excellence – giving prominence to the stakeholder voice

The LSC Framework for Excellence (FfE) was introduced in Chapter 1. The declared intention of the framework is to provide information for learners and those supporting them, such as their parents and guardians, to enable them to make informed choices. This information includes the views of other learners, the quality of provision, including facilities and resources, and whether learners' needs are being met.

The LSC website provides a review of its early use, noting that, *The FfE has been strongly influenced by experience from piloting and feedback from providers and stakeholders during implementation.* From 2009, the LSC claimed to have made the framework simpler and more sensitive to the diverse nature of the sector. There were nine indicators, differentiated between 'core' and 'specific' according to their relevance to particular types of provider and provision.

Consideration of Table 6.1 will show just how powerful the learner voice is: it is given equal weighting alongside what the learners achieve (success rates) and where they go on to (learner destinations). It is also an indicator that, unlike matters pertaining to the finances of an organisation, is published. So the message here, in terms of reputation management, might well be that it is not enough for your learners to do well and make progress, they have to say they have been well taught and have enjoyed the experience.

Category	Indicator	Core or specific	Published or unpublished
Learner and qualification success	Success rates	Core	Published
Learner views	Learner views	Core	Published
Learner destinations	Learner destinations (including a statement of volume of employment outcomes)	Core	Published
Responsiveness to employers	Employer views	Specific	Published
	Amount of training (statement of volume for information; not graded)	Specific	Published
	Training Quality Standard	Specific	Published
Financial health and management	Financial health	Specific	Unpublished
	Financial management and control evaluation	Specific	Unpublished
Resource efficiency	Funding per successful outcome	Core	Unpublished

Table 6.1: Framework for Excellence indicators for 2009/10

In addition to 'Learner views', another significant category by which provision is judged is that of 'Responsiveness to employers'. Here again, the indicator, 'Employer views' will be published. It was the intention of the LSC that the Framework would provide a consistent rating of providers, so that employers are able to factor this into their decision-making process and that Skills Brokers (staff employed to facilitate use of initiatives such as Train to Gain) would use the Framework scores to support recommendations to employers in terms of where they contracted their training provision.

It was a further expectation of the LSC that colleges and providers would be able to use the Framework to assess and improve their own performance and incorporate the findings of self-assessment into reports for governing bodies and boards. The thrust was towards making all providers use common measures and so develop a more reliable capacity to self-assess and to support continuous improvement.

The LSC when advocating the Framework sought to sell it to the sector with the following claims.

- *The Framework will facilitate coherence and the integration of processes across the sector; it will develop a common perspective among colleges and providers on what should be measured and how.*
- *The Framework will enable colleges and providers to demonstrate excellence where it already exists and help to develop it.*
- *The move will be a major step on the journey to self-regulation.*
- *The Framework offers the capacity to target underperformance and manage performance risk.*
- *Costs and burdens on providers are being minimised by using existing data and systems wherever possible.*

(LSC, 2009)

There are further statements regarding how the Framework would be used, specifically by the LSC itself and by Ofsted. The LSC would use the Framework when determining support, interaction, funding and measuring whether or not a provider was delivering value for money. (This function has now been taken over by the SFA, one of the two bodies replacing the LSC.) Ofsted would use the Framework's scores to inform its judgement against the criteria for risk assessment, which in turn would determine the urgency and/or priority of a provider for inspection and also the degree of the inspection's intervention.

Given that 'Learner views' and 'Responsiveness to employers' are two out of the six published criteria, and given the prominence that the Framework is intended to enjoy, then it becomes an all-too-obvious imperative for providers to engage with the learner voice. If your funding and inspection regime is going to be dependent on what learners say about the teaching, their progress, the learning materials and the wider provider resources, then it would be a foolish management team to treat this lightly. And what management teams want will travel down to the line to become what teachers must do.

PRACTICAL TASK PRACTICAL TASK PRACTICAL TASK PRACTICAL TASK PRACTICAL TASK

Ask your mentor/coach or line manager what they know about the Framework for Evidence and ask them if they can get a copy of the published reports for 'Learner views' and 'Responsiveness to employers'.

If they are available, read them and discuss them with your colleague – it might motivate them to read the reports for the first time! If the reports are not readily available, or your colleague seems reluctant to pursue them, you might want to reflect on why this might be.

Discerning the learner voice

CASE STUDY
'3 out of 10 on the BBS'
Back in 1988, I had started teaching A level psychology. It was a small group and the majority were in their early twenties rather than the more typical 16–19 cohort we might expect today.

Most had been at the college at least a year, working their way up from the recently introduced GCSEs to A levels. I got on well with the group and enjoyed what I did. After one session, Joe said, 'That was good today: only a three on the BBS.' 'What's the BBS?' I asked. 'The B******** Boredom Scale. He's the most boring teacher we have so we rate everybody else by his standards. The lower the number the better the lesson.' (To protect those involved, I can''t reveal the name behind the acronym even after all these years.)

Much amused and slightly flattered I left the classroom.

What might we learn from this? That students have opinions of their teachers? No surprise really. But that they actually had a scoring system and one – though making harsh use of my eponymous colleague – that actually worked because it provided a benchmark, a measure of consistency that could be applied and understood, was arguably ahead of its time. The point was that the teacher in question did rather go on and on in the staffroom in a lugubrious tone and without variation in pace or pedantry. The classroom was obviously the same. The feedback provided to all teachers was the students' way of motivating us, challenging us, amusing us: maybe all of those things. But – and because at the time student surveys, teaching evaluations, Ofsted and the like were nothing more that a bad dream in someone's imagination – it did represent one of my earliest experiences of the student voice.

However, given the way the college was managed and the narrowness of the curriculum offered there were no evaluation processes and hence no quality improvement channels left to the students other than to tease and chide us with this scale. For the students it was a case of sticking with the subject, motivating themselves for the exam and hoping for better things in the future. And how many of us have suffered mediocre or uninspiring teaching only to reminisce with friends years later and hear that nothing changed?

This is not an argument for some of the more extreme versions of the student voice that we will explore later in this chapter where tenure can effectively been cancelled by low 'grades' awarded by students to teaching staff. It is to note that, while students may have an opinion, there will be little or no systematic quality improvement unless the student voice is captured, feedback evaluated in an informed way and effective development targets and plans put in place.

First point of contact in the evaluation cycle

In most organisations there is an immediate way of listening to your consumers, your customers, and that is to make yourself available and talk to them. This seems to be something that many teachers avoid – understandably perhaps in the context of heavy timetabling and rushing from class to class – but it seems something that teachers rarely build into their lessons. Granted, we may be teaching lively, even volatile young adults (and sometimes older ones) and there is perhaps a fear that to talk about how things are going is to somehow sacrifice the 'authority' of the teacher and to belittle your own status and expertise. But remember, this is lifelong learning we are working in and the most effective teaching and learning strategies continue to be shown to be those that ask for and create effective engagement between teacher and learner.

You need a careful approach: the course specification is not negotiable, the timing of exams and course work is set, reports to parents and employers are required, so avoid giving the impression that the classroom has become a market place in which learning can be bartered. But do not, under any circumstances, avoid getting informal feedback from your learners and acting on it. They may comment about being bored, about a particular topic not being relevant or seeming difficult: listen, discuss, respond. Yes, this is extra work but in my experience most learners will cut you more slack if you have tried to listen and improve things than if they feel they have just been ignored. We cannot hide the fact that the litigation culture enthusiastically promoted over the last 20 years has led to a situation where too many people's response is to complain rather than to enquire, to seek redress rather then begin a dialogue, to blame rather than to reflect. In this climate you want to have your learners on your side because should there be one unhappy voice, with an axe to grind, you will very much welcome the support and endorsement of the majority of the group should any complaint be formalised. And besides, it's good practice: you really can learn a lot about your teaching by talking to your learners.

Even if you do practise this, your organisation is likely to have some formal and evaluation procedures that it will want you to adopt and employ so it is appropriate to consider some examples of these now.

Approaches to structured evaluation: philosophy, tools, implementation

Philosophy

There are three problems with commonly found approaches to student evaluation. The first is the philosophy, the second the tools and the third the implementation. To rework Abraham Lincoln somewhat: *Evaluation should be of the learners, by the learners, for the learners*. In my experience, it is all too often of the learners, by the teacher, for the management.

In terms of a philosophy, it is likely that approaches to evaluation and to capturing the student voice were set in train back in the 1990s and may well have remained unaltered. Those responsible for setting up the policy and procedure may well now be retired and those inheriting their efforts may genuinely adopt an 'if it ain't broke, don't fix it' strategy. The problem is that few actually ask the question about whether it ever worked properly in the first place.

The critical concept here is that of 'ownership'. If the approach to evaluation within your organisation does not encourage your engagement and your enthusiasm to improve, if quality assurance is not personalised at each teacher's level then, in our experience, there is every likelihood that data will be collected, published and ignored or collected, published and considered to abstruse levels of complexity to the point that it might as well have been ignored because little or no clear improvements can be identified and applied.

There are different ways to exercise different evaluation strategies. You can capture feedback directly from learners about the teacher and the topic; you can capture the bigger picture about a course or programme, perhaps consisting of different cohorts at different venues; you can ask the whole student body for its opinion about the whole college and curriculum. The small- versus large-scale approach is seen clearly in the tools chosen to capture the learner voice.

Tools

Subject/module evaluation

Here the level of evaluation is at topic and teacher level. The collection of feedback from participants may be informal, e.g. by the use of 'happy sheets' where learners simply mark their opinion on a row of smiley faces, or you may make use of sticky notes, to be stuck to the wall or board on the way out, allowing the learner to comment on what was successfully learned or not, how they enjoyed the lesson or not, and so on.

These simple tools are worth considering because they can give you a very early warning signal about how the class is progressing in terms of individual learning and satisfaction and engagement. However, they may lack validity and reliability so should be used sparingly; and if used there must be some follow-up, some response at the teacher level, otherwise learners will swiftly disengage and cease to give the activity any value.

Many organisations will have adopted a more formal style of evaluation at the subject/module level. There are usually two types, a 'Learning Questionnaire', which should have a specific focus on the learning experience, and a 'Reactionnaire', which is more likely to have a focus on the course but also on more peripheral aspects such as parking, rooming, refreshments, etc.

In terms of completing these types of surveys you will most likely find the Likert scale or Bipolar scale approaches helpful.

Likert

Using the scale please indicate your response to each statement:

1 = strongly agree 2 = agree 3 = disagree 4 = strongly disagree

My understanding of the topic has increased   [2]

My ability to apply new skills has improved   [3]

And so on.

Bipolar

Please mark on the scale your response:

The lessons were well organised	1	2	3	4	5	The lessons were not well organised
The explanations were clear	1	2	3	4	5	The explanations were not clear

And so on.

Both these types of evaluation questionnaires may be supplemented with space to add comments.

Another approach is to provide themes and ask for an open, written response. For example:

Please let us know your opinion of the following elements in your course:

1. Recruitment and induction … .

2. Teaching and learning … .

3. Assessment and feedback … .

Whichever approach is adopted, and early on in your career you are more likely to be obliged to use what is provided than be trusted with generating your own tools, there are certain key principles that should be evident. In either the actual document or in your explanation accompanying its use, ensure that the following are addressed.

- Clearly explain the purpose.
- Make it clear whether the questionnaire is anonymous.
- Use brief and clear language.
- Encourage honest responses.
- Make sure the format and layout produces something easy to follow and visually attractive.
- Avoid multiple themes/topics within one question.

Figure 6.1 is a copy of the Module Evaluation we used with our students in 2009/10. We believed it was already an improvement from the earlier version, as that ran to 30 questions, including several topics not related to actually teaching the module (e.g. course organisation, library resources, additional support) but we're sure it could be improved further.

REFLECTIVE TASK

Study the Module Evaluation form (Figure 6.1). Make a note of whether you think it would provide the information a teacher would need to improve the quality of their work with the next group of learners. Is it clear what you have to do? How would you feel if you were asked to fill it in six times (once for each module on the course) as a student? How would you feel if your learners were filling it about *your* teaching? Any other response?

PRACTICAL TASK   PRACTICAL TASK   PRACTICAL TASK   PRACTICAL TASK   PRACTICAL TASK

If you are reading this book as a trainee teacher working towards QTLS, ask your mentor for copies of subject/module evaluation questionnaires that are used in the department. Perhaps you can ask to see the feedback collected in the last academic year and any action plans that were produced as a result. Discuss with your mentor if there are any aspects of the evaluation that you need to be particularly aware of during your professional practice.

Course programme evaluation

One obvious way of evaluating the overall course or programme is to scrutinise all the subject/modules evaluations. But a moment's reflection will indicate that there are more

PCET   Module Evaluation

Module Code and Title: ....

| 1 = strongly agree | 2 = agree | 3 = disagree | 4 = strongly disagree |

CURRICULUM		1	2	3	4
1.	The learning outcomes and content of the module were made clear at the start of the module and were effectively addressed				
2.	The sessions included relevant and current examples of theory, practice, research and policy				
TEACHING AND LEARNING					
3.	A range of teaching strategies were used that met my learning needs				
4.	The sessions were interesting/informative				
5.	I was encouraged to reflect on personal and/or professional experience				
6.	I was encouraged to participate in discussion and contribute ideas				
7.	The skills I was expected to use and develop were clearly stated				
8.	The materials provided supported my learning				
9.	The sessions provided models of a high standard of teaching and learning				
10.	The extent of personal responsibility for my own learning was made clear				
ASSESSMENT AND ACHIEVEMENT					
11.	Effective guidance was provided on how the assessed work would be marked				
12.	Support for assessment was provided or signposted				
13.	Assessment allowed me to identify links between theory and practice				
STUDENT SUPPORT AND GUIDANCE					
14.	The tutor/s was/were approachable and I felt able to discuss any issues associated with the module				
15.	Information about progression from this to other modules was made clear (as appropriate course calendar)				

I particularly valued .....

Observations, concerns and/or suggestions for improvement

Please complete your course information:

PGCE / Cert HE	Full Time / Part Time	Year 1 / 2
Centre:		
Module Tutor		

Figure 6.1: Example of a module evaluation form

aspects to a course than those for which an individual teacher might be responsible or might be able to influence the quality.

REFLECTIVE TASK

REFLECTIVE TASK

Think about the range of provisions, resources and activities that, if provided correctly, constitute effective and satisfying participation in a course and, if not, frequently appear on learner complaint forms.

You may have listed the induction and registration, library/learning services, learning support, catering, car parking, recreational facilities, fees, litter, behaviour of other students, etc. These are important, but need to be recognised as being separate from a focus on teaching and learning in the classroom or workshop.

One way forward is to make use of a more broadly focused questionnaire, more in keeping with the reactionnaires described above. However, given that this may well be issued towards the end of a course (otherwise some things to be evaluated may not have actually happened yet), there is often a downturn in the number of learners completing such questionnaires and certainly little or no opportunity for any feedback to inform and improve delivery of the programme during the year.

One development that addresses the need to gain an overall student perspective of a course – and one that is more current – has been the use of Student Consultative groups. Here, a cohort of learners will meet regularly with a course leader or with staff from the teaching team. There may be some negotiation and possibly selection as to how many represent the group and who they will be. Within the broad curriculum that is lifelong learning there may be some groups of learners who will not be able to confidently express their student voice and in these situations one or more advocates may need to be found.

Our experience has been that such groups need to be properly convened, well briefed and appropriately managed if they are to be useful in providing an effective evaluation and quality improvement process.

- Properly convened means that all members of the group must understand the purpose of the consultative meeting in terms of the student voice. They are neither effective nor representative if they are hijacked by one or two learners with their 'own agenda'. (Just because that's a cliché doesn't mean it's not true!)
- Well briefed means that if, for the sake of efficiency, representatives are nominated to speak on behalf of the group, they need to understand their role and to have properly managed time to meet with the group in advance and capture their ideas and comments for feeding to the meeting.
- Appropriately managed means that the person chairing the meeting must work through an agenda that has a real focus on quality: and that includes what is done well and what might be in need of improvement. It is essential to convey a genuine sense of listening to the learner voice but all parties must understand that this is to seek improvement, not just to grumble and moan or defend and deny.

Above all, the timescale and lines of reporting of any such meeting must be clear and appropriate. There must be transparency and integrity in what is fed back to consultative groups in terms of feasible and realistic outcomes. It is ineffective and probably more damaging to make optimistic promises that are not within the gift of the classroom teacher, the course team or even the head of department. While it is not always easy dealing with feedback from disappointed learners who seem easily dissatisfied, the rash promise of 'I'll sort it out for you' may only be storing up bigger problems because further perceived failures within an organisation, particularly where solutions have been promised, tend to inflame grievances further. If you are involved in these sort of consultative meetings early on in your career, ensure you are not without the support of more experienced colleagues.

Implementation

The actual implementation of whatever evaluation tools are chosen brings us to one of the most contentious aspects of the whole process, what we call ownership. As in the question posed in the introduction, for whose benefit are we undertaking the evaluation: the learner, the teacher, the organisation? Well, the ideal answer would be for all three but we need to examine this more closely.

To do so, let's consider an established and successful approach to evaluation, that of Kirkpatrick's Four Levels[TM] Evaluation Model. The origins of Kirkpatrick's model are from employment-based training where an improvement in knowledge and application and subsequent performance and productivity is the desired goal. It can, however, be equally well applied to educational settings and offers an effective template for considering

Kirkpatrick's Four Levels[TM] Evaluation Model

As Tamkin *et al*. (2002) report, Kirkpatrick's Four Levels[TM] Evaluation Model is a long-established and well-regarded model of evaluation. Its pre-eminent feature is to recognise that to fully appreciate the impact, particularly the benefits, of an educational or training experience then something other than just an immediate capture of participant opinion will be necessary. Kirkpatrick proposes four levels of evaluation:

1. Reaction – what the learner thought about the teaching/training.
2. Learning – the resulting increase in knowledge or capability of the learner.
3. Behaviour – the extent of behaviour and capability improvement and how the learner implements this in their role.
4. Results – the effects on the business or environment resulting from the learner's performance.

Where Kirkpatrick's model has been shown to be most effective is where the evaluation has been continued through all four levels; but here the increasing complexity is accompanied by increasing cost, one of the reasons a full application of the model is not always seen.

There is an argument, drawn from direct personal experience of evaluation strategies and from the reports from many of our students, that there is very evident and compelling variation in the concept of ownership of the process and the outcomes of evaluation.

Ownership of the outcomes

At one extreme, we know of the documentary evidence being required to be handed over directly to senior staff, with those teachers involved not being party to any personal scrutiny, interpretation or discussion of the feedback received or the drawing-up of any action plans through which to respond. It doesn't mean there are no action plans, but that these may be imposed without agreement from line managers and above. This might have involved evaluation at Levels 1 and 2, that is direct reactions from the students and evidence of learning as shown through success rates (see Chapter 5), which can be valuable information for teachers for their professional reflection and personal development.

However, the perception is that in some organisations so long as the evaluations are providing the right sort of data for the SFA, Ofsted (or any other inspection regime), or for some nice headline in the local press, then there is little in the way of institutional support for teachers wishing to personally and professionally reflect and seek to improve other than expecting them to do so.

How do we solve this scenario? Take ownership of the process and make copies of the evaluation questionnaires (of whatever format) before handing the originals over. You need to know now what your learners think, not wait for the publication (or otherwise) of an institutional report.

A different problem is where the process of carrying out evaluations might be genuinely allowed to rest with those teachers involved but where it lacks independent scrutiny. We know of reports where the consequences of performativity and the culture of targets have an impact on the integrity of the data collection in its first stage, where teachers are scared of the slightest negative-looking feedback, either in words or numbers. Let's just say the sampling process might need tightening up.

How do we solve this problem? Don't run away from it: as we said in the introductory chapter get comfortable with your data. The figures might show that 10% of your students didn't think the lessons were effectively organised. But if only ten people hand the evaluation sheet back in, this would be one person. And maybe you know something about them: they are very hard to please, they don't pay attention to what they are asked to do, they transferred from another course and haven't been happy about it all year. There could be any number of reasons why the feedback is not positive, but the best teachers know the learner and know the reason, and use this to explain and deflect any management criticisms rather than hide it.

On the other hand, perhaps the feedback is not too positive and there are not many mitigating factors. Take a good hard look at what the feedback says, reflect on it, develop an action plan, talk to your mentor, to other trusted colleagues and be honest enough to accept you need to improve. As Gary Player, one of the leading golfers of the 1960s and 70s, is reported as saying when accused of being lucky: 'the harder I practise the luckier I get'.

Final thoughts – to embrace or avoid?

The overall point is this: some evaluation of your students' experiences will be undertaken. You can decide how far you want to engage with this, but it *will* happen.

If you feel a bureaucratic approach is over-intrusive and intent on producing evidence to paint a good picture rather than help you improve, then undertake your own informal evaluations. Capture student opinion (Kirkpatrick Level 1) by discussion or simple feedback sheets and use more informed evidence such as Value Added or Distance Travelled (Kirkpatrick Level 2) to judge how your own students have done in their learning, using more individual and informed data than just, for example, relying on success rates.

If you find yourself in a department where the processes are balanced and effective, but none of the teaching team seem keen to own the outcomes and act on them, then you must at least ensure that you do. If you are working towards a teaching qualification and subsequent QTLS status, you will have to provide evidence of this, regardless of what colleagues are doing.

Don't hide from feedback from your learners: gather it well and use it confidently. If you are engaged in a performance review or appraisal process then take your evaluations and proposed action plan to these meetings. Be confident in the quality of your work by demonstrating exactly how you evaluate it and improve it – you might find your manager is impressed!

The search for effective evaluation in the sector has been around for some time. Over 25 years ago Donald (1984) set out the scene and proposed some strategies that were fairly low key and non-intrusive. Clearly, the policy and processes have moved on: however, our point is that while there may be need to debate about the instruments used to capture the learner voice, that debate is something that will be in the background. From the point of view of the relatively new practitioner it is not as important as what is done with the outcomes of such processes because these outcomes will be there and they will be published.

So, what you need to engage with is policy and process that effectively merge into an evaluation strategy that can genuinely facilitate improvement, be it of teaching, assessment, resources, etc.

A SUMMARY OF **KEY POINTS**

In this chapter we have:

> **considered the identity of the learner voice;**

> **identified and examined the key indicators of quality assurance that are considered when taking the views of learners into account;**

> **advocated the need for your ownership of the evaluation tools chosen and for engagement with the outcomes;**

> **offered support in interpreting the feedback you receive from your learners so as to place it in the appropriate context;**

> **advised that, as a new teacher in the sector, consideration of the learner voice will not be optional.**

REFERENCES REFERENCES REFERENCES REFERENCES REFERENCES REFERENCES

Donald, A (1984) Evaluation in Further Education – Towards a Solution. *Journal of Vocational Education & Training*, 36 (94): 53–8.

LSC (2006) *Framework for Excellence*. http://readingroom.lsc.gov.uk/lsc/NationalFramework _for_ Excellence_consultation_doc_July_06.pdf (accessed 2010).

LSC (2009) *Framework for Excellence: Unified Post-16 Performance Assessment*. http://readingroom.lsc.gov.uk/lsc/National/FfE_Unified_Post-16.pdf (accessed 2010).

Tamkin P, Yarnall, J, and Kerrin, M (2002) *Kirkpatrick and Beyond: A Review of Models of Training Evaluation.* Brighton: Institute for Employment Studies.

Websites

Businessballs www.businessballs.com

Learning and Skills Network www.lsnlearning.org.uk

Learning and Skills Improvement Service www.lsis.org.uk

Kirkpartick Partners www.kirkpatrickpartners.com

National Student Survey www.thestudentsurvey.com

Teacher Net www.teachernet.gov.uk

7
Culture, ethos and values

This chapter is designed to:

- provide you with a clear understanding of the culture of organisations in the lifelong learning sector;
- discuss attitudes and beliefs and their effect on the culture of an organisation;
- consider inclusion and differentiation in the lifelong learning sector;
- focus on how you can promote a positive ethos and culture in your organisation.

It addresses the following Professional Standards for QTLS:

AS 7 Improving the quality of their practice.

AP 5.1 Communicate and collaborate with colleagues and/or others, within and outside the organisation, to enhance learners' experience.

It also addresses the Level 5 DTTLS module: Continuing personal and professional development.

Introduction: the college/organisation culture

Wise teachers 'steer the boat' by using the rudder in the back; they do not need to be at the prow to influence the direction being taken.

(Adapted from Nagel, 1998, page 197)

When we talk about ethos and values in educational organisations, we first need to try to define what we mean by the culture of the organisation. The culture of the college can be said to be the predominating attitudes and behaviour that characterise the functioning of the organisation. These include the attitudes and beliefs of persons both inside the college and in the external environment. These are the cultural norms of the college and are evidenced by the relationships between persons in the college. Each of these factors may present barriers to change or be a significant factor in the creation of a positive ethos.

PRACTICAL TASK PRACTICAL TASK PRACTICAL TASK PRACTICAL TASK PRACTICAL TASK

- Draw an image that sums up the culture of your organisation.
- If your college was a car what would it be?
- List six adjectives that describe your organisational culture.
- Are these adjectives positive or negative or a mixture of both? What does this say about your organisation?

The impact of culture

An examination of culture is important because each college has an ambience or culture of its own and this can affect the performance of that college. Depending upon how well leaders understand and use this notion, culture can assist improvement efforts for at-risk students, or act as a barrier to change. When organisations seek to improve, a focus on the values, beliefs, and norms of both the college and the environment outside is necessary.

Culture can play an enormous part in the recruitment, retention and achievement of learners and the length of time staff stay at an organisation. If a college keeps its staff for a long time and recruits the siblings of existing students it could be seen as an indication of the positive culture and ethos of the organisation.

Attitudes and beliefs

The attitudes and beliefs of key people in a college shape that culture. Each new principal will endeavour to bring about a change to the culture of the organisation to be in line with their own attitudes and beliefs. When there is conflict with the attitudes and beliefs of other key influential players in the organisation there may be problems.

A college is a complex organisation by itself, as well as being part of a larger national picture. Frequently, the individual's understanding of the national picture serves as a basis for maintaining the status quo and opposing change. Anticipating trouble in relation to the national picture is characteristic of many staff. They can decide that it is not worth changing as frequent changes made by successive governments renders their efforts useless.

The internally held mental attitudes and beliefs of teachers regarding teaching, students and change impact on the behaviour of teachers towards students, especially those at risk. This is particularly important, because identifying and confronting beliefs that prohibit students from achieving their potential are vital components of college improvement efforts.

These attitudes also influence teachers' responses to proposed college improvements or initiatives. Resolving fears and anxiety created by change is a major task for those leading organisations. Taking time to ensure that the reasons for the change, the practicality of the change, and the philosophical basis for the effort are well understood by everyone involved will enhance the likelihood of lasting implementation.

PRACTICAL TASK PRACTICAL TASK PRACTICAL TASK PRACTICAL TASK PRACTICAL TASK

- If you were in a position to do so, what would you choose to change in your organisation, and what would you choose to celebrate?
- What would a teacher recently appointed to your organisation say about its culture?
- What would a teacher with eight years' experience in the organisation say about it? Why might their view be different?
- What would students say about it?

Cultural norms

Just as the attitudes and beliefs of persons both inside and outside the college building may facilitate or impede change, so do the norms, or informal rules, that govern behaviour exert influence on change efforts. These norms are developed over time and are influenced by the attitudes and beliefs of those inside and outside the college. In turn, the norms define expectations regarding how things are to be done. This process exerts an influence on beliefs and attitudes as well as personal relationships.

A widely shared vision

A norm of protecting what is important evolves from a shared vision of what things are important. A shared vision among students, teachers, parents, and the external community is a feature of the colleges in which all students are most likely to succeed academically. If this shared sense of purpose exists, members of the college community are able to spell out what constitutes good performance in a relatively precise and consistent way. Without a shared vision, students, teachers, administrators, and parents may not know what is expected of them.

Relationships

Just as the attitudes and beliefs of persons both inside and outside the college affect change and the norms of the organisation, relationships between persons and groups of persons are part of the culture that can either facilitate or impede change. The relationships teachers have with each other, their students, and the community affect the culture of the organisation. Similarly, the relationships between students and their peers, teachers, and the college as a whole can help or hinder improvement efforts.

When teachers are interested in students and demonstrate respect for them, a community of caring is nurtured. This community sense reduces isolation and alienation. When many students feel this sense of community, their need for positive relationships with adults and group membership may be satisfied in ways that mesh the student culture with the organisation's culture in positive ways.

Example

I worked at a local college for ten years and came to love the college and the students who studied there. The culture and ethos of the organisation is difficult to explain but it is like a warm, friendly pair of arms that goes around all who enter the organisation. We used to call it the 'student experience' and, without thinking very much about what exactly it was, we knew that our students had a different experience to most others.

In my time there we never got a grade 1 from Ofsted, or outstanding results, or national acclaim but we maintained an inclusive, non-violent environment – in spite of serious racial tension in the locality.

Today, as soon as you enter the buildings you can see that students are happy, laughing and enjoying themselves. The walls are lined with pictures of students past and present, telling their stories and celebrating their successes.

The staff operate an open-door policy and there are many enrichment opportunities to add value to the student experience. The college is quite small as colleges go and everyone knows everyone else and takes equal responsibility for students' welfare.

Year on year students follow their siblings after hearing them talking about their experiences and word of mouth brings in many more. They talk about the college as a safe place that cares about them and helps them to succeed. The students do not care so much about results or league tables; they just know that if the college could help their brother/sister/friend then it is the place for them.

As time has passed and I have started teaching about leadership and management, every time I come to talk about culture I talk about the 'student experience' at this college and describe it as a VW camper van – with flowers on the sides. It is a bit rickety but everyone is welcome and it gets you to where you want to go and you have a lot of fun on the way!

Ethos and values

Ethos can be defined as the distinctive character, spirit and attitudes of a people, culture, era, etc. or the disposition, character or fundamental values peculiar to a specific person, people, culture or movement.

We can see then that the culture of an organisation is concerned with the ways of working or the way of life, whereas the ethos is the character or spirit of the organisation, which can be personified by the values of the staff and students in the organisation.

To further investigate this concept of culture it is possible to consider the framework expounded by Deal and Kennedy (1982). According to Lumby (2001) they asserted that the culture of an organisation is defined by the following indicators.

- Shared values and beliefs.
- Heroes and heroines.
- Ritual.
- Ceremony.
- Stories.
- Informal network of cultural players.

Taking each of these indicators in turn it becomes clear from whence the culture of any organisation derive.

Shared values and beliefs

These can underpin an organisation to such an extent that they need not be explicit. Lumby (2001) suggests that shared values are the provider of the culture of an educational organisation. In most organisations these 'shared' values may not always be in complete harmony. Some people or departments may have different shared values. In fact, the concept must be considered that there can be more than one culture coexisting in an organisation.

Heroes and heroines

The values shared by the members of an organisation are often demonstrated in what are commonly referred to as its 'heroes and heroines'. In other words, in the beliefs and behaviour of those members who are honoured and respected in the organisation for the manner in which they do their job. Such heroes are often focused on the student. For example, there is often a high regard for lecturers who work hard to offer excellent teaching and learning in the face of increasing workloads. Their achievements are seen as heroic and are to be emulated.

Rituals, ceremonies and stories

These three indicators share many common features. They describe the methods in which the educational organisation chooses to support and celebrate the ethos or culture of the organisation. This can be seen clearly in the annual graduations, the end-of-term celebrations, the awarding of prizes and the celebration of individual and team success.

Network of players

The final indicator of culture is the network of players, those who are the influencers and the storytellers. These people, usually the managers themselves, influence the culture of the organisation by their personalities and their determination to move in a certain direction.

Sub-cultures

It would be unrealistic to presume that in a large college or organisation there was just one culture. It would be more accurate to consider that within large organisations, such as FE colleges, there is a number of 'sub-cultures' that coexist.

Sub-cultures are important and can add value to an organisation if the sub-culture is a positive one that maintains the values of the dominant culture. This type of sub-culture might be seen in certain departments which are very competitive and ambitious. They might embrace the culture of the organisation but observe it in a more extreme and fervent way.

Secondly, there is another type of sub-culture in which the group accept the dominant culture of the organisation but also concurrently hold their own values linked directly to their occupation.

Finally, there is the type of sub-culture that opposes the values of the dominant culture and holds its own, opposing values. In most colleges you can find examples of each of these sub-cultures and each in its own way can influence the overall ethos of the organisation.

PRACTICAL TASK PRACTICAL TASK PRACTICAL TASK PRACTICAL TASK PRACTICAL TASK

Consider your own team, department, faculty and organisation – are these sub-cultures and, if so, what type are they?
How, if at all, do they affect the success of the organisation?

CASE STUDY
By Alex, curriculum quality manager
As a cross-college manager working to raise the standards of teaching and learning across the college I have worked with many teams and departments. I would describe the culture of the organisation as student-focused and success-driven. However, within various departments a variety of sub-cultures exist.

Sport – This department adopts the culture of the organisation but uses it to push students and staff to achieve excellence. They are extremely competitive and want to be the most successful department in the college and to enable their students to win in the competitive sporting environment.

Preuniformed services – This department also adopts the culture of the organisation but very much as it relates to their vocational area. They have very formal discipline systems and focus on preparing young people for a life in the uniformed services. They also focus on competition but use techniques that are possibly against the organisation's cultural beliefs in order to mimic the behaviours that exist in their vocational area. The staff and students are very formal and disciplined but successful and student-focused.

A level studies – This department holds its own culture that is not in line with the culture of the college as a whole. They believe that students should be independent and self-focused and should have little help from staff to support their learning. The staff are remote from the students and interested in academic success rather than the whole experience of the student. There is little offered to students to enhance their experiences and the whole focus is on progression to university.

None of these sub-cultures is wrong and all are successful in their own way. However, we can see that the overall culture of the organisation is influenced by these sub-cultures as is the experience of the students.

How do we share our ethos?

PRACTICAL TASK PRACTICAL TASK **PRACTICAL TASK** PRACTICAL TASK **PRACTICAL TASK**

- Think about your organisation's mission statement.
- Does this mission statement reflect the culture of your organisation?
- Where is your organisation's mission statement displayed?
- Who knows (about) it?
- What happens if you fulfil/live up to the mission statement?
- What happens if you don't?

The key to sharing our ethos and values is communication. All organisations need to communicate to staff, students, parents, governors and the community what its ethos and values are, and what is expected of them when they engage with the organisation.

Why communications skills are so important

The purpose of communication is to get your message across to others. This is a process that involves both the sender of the message and the receiver. This process leaves room for error, with messages often misinterpreted by one or more of the parties involved. This causes unnecessary confusion and counter-productivity. In fact, a message is successful only when both the sender and the receiver perceive it in the same way.

By successfully getting your message across, you convey your thoughts and ideas effectively. When not successful, the thoughts and ideas that you convey do not necessarily reflect your own, causing a communications breakdown and creating roadblocks that stand in the way of your goals – both personally and professionally. This is what happens in organisations that don't have a clear understanding of their common goals and values.

Getting your message across is paramount if you are to progress. To do this, you must understand what your message is, what audience you are sending it to, and how it will be perceived. You must also weigh-in the circumstances surrounding your communications, such as situational and cultural context.

Communications skills – the importance of removing barriers

Communication barriers can pop up at every stage of the communication process – which consists of **sender**, **message**, **channel**, **receiver**, **feedback** and **context** – and have the potential to create misunderstanding and confusion.

To be an effective communicator and to get your point across without misunderstanding and confusion, your goal should be to lessen the frequency of these barriers at each stage of this process with clear, concise, accurate, well-planned communications. We follow the process through below.

Sender
As an organisation you want to communicate your goals and values to your staff, students and stakeholders. You want to send a clear unambiguous message that can be easily understood and you want to reinforce it within all of your future communications.

Message
Written, oral and non-verbal communications are affected by the sender's tone, method of organisation, validity of the argument, what is communicated and what is left out, as well as your individual style of communicating. Messages also have intellectual and emotional components, with intellect allowing us the ability to reason and emotion allowing us to present motivational appeals, ultimately changing minds and actions. Spending time getting the message right before communication is vital to success in communicating that message. This is why organisations spend so much time designing their mission statements, publicity materials and websites.

Channel
Messages are conveyed through channels, both verbal, including face-to-face meetings, telephone and videoconferencing, and written, including letters, emails, memos and reports. Many organisations have newsletters for staff and students in order to communicate their messages and to celebrate and showcase their culture and values.

Receiver
These messages are delivered to an audience. The audience also enters into the communication process with ideas and feelings that will undoubtedly influence their understanding of the message and their response. It is important to get the communication right for the respective audience. This may mean changing language or tone in order to appeal to different audience's needs.

Feedback

Your audience will provide you with feedback, verbal and non-verbal reactions to your communicated message. Paying close attention to this feedback is crucial to ensuring the audience understood the message and are able to buy into the culture of the organisation.

Context

The situation in which your message is delivered is the context. This may include the surrounding environment or broader culture and may influence your choice of medium or the message you want to communicate.

Celebrating success

One of the key ways of communicating the culture of an organisation is by creating an environment that celebrates the success of its students and staff. I have visited many colleges over the years and those that have a culture of celebrating success are the most inviting to visitors.

When you enter a building and see displays of students' work and photographs of students' successes you immediately feel that this is a place that you can do well in. Prospective students and their parents will feel that they too can do well and be celebrated in their turn.

Awards such as 'student of the month' or 'teacher of the month' go a long way towards motivating and celebrating people''s achievements in a climate where they might not necessarily be rewarded economically.

At a college in which I was working, I was nominated by my peers to receive a 'star' award for my hard work during the year and was given a bouquet of flowers and some vouchers at the end-of-year staff development day. This was very special to me because my colleagues had recognised my work and the college had celebrated it in a very public way. I still have my 'star' shoes bought with the vouchers. Whenever I wear them I remember the college and the feeling of being celebrated.

Becoming a community

The terms 'widening participation', 'differentiation' and 'inclusive practice' are commonplace in the lifelong learning sector. The sector prides itself on its work in opening up opportunities for accessing education and training to a diverse population of learners.

These concepts are defined as follows:

- 'Widening participation' is a process by which education and training providers take steps to recruit, and then provide ongoing support for, learners, who due to their social, economic or ethnic backgrounds, are less likely to take part in education and training.
- 'Differentiation' is an approach to teaching and learning that both recognises the individuality of learners and also informs ways of planning for learning and teaching that take these individualities into consideration.
- 'Inclusive practice' is an approach to teaching and learning that endeavours to encourage the fullest participation of learners and that recognises and respects equality and diversity.

These three distinct concepts complement each other. Widening participation will encourage an increasingly diverse learner population that will display a variety of different needs, and will engender an inclusive approach to planning for learning and teaching.

We might say that inclusion is clearly about opening up access to education and training opportunities, but it is equally about how students experience that education and training.

There are two approaches to coping with the inclusion agenda:

1. To try to help all learners to fit into the educational contexts they encounter.
2. To try to adjust the educational environment to be more suitable to all the learners whose needs it is intended to address.

The second approach would be generally considered the most suitable. This is all the more achievable if we think how best to design our learning environments to address the five factors that underpin successful learning. In other words, inclusive teaching could be defined along the lines of responding as follows:

1. Doing everything we can to enhance the 'want' to learn.
2. Clarifying the 'need' to learn, as identified in the curriculum.
3. Adjusting the 'learning by doing' tasks and activities we use with learners, to allow all learners to have suitable opportunities to join in.
4. Maximising the 'feedback' that learners gain from us and each other.
5. Helping all learners to 'make sense' or 'digest' the information they encounter.

To achieve these aims we need to seek feedback from our learners about their experience of our teaching and their individual experience of learning in the context of their own particular needs. Learning is done by individuals. Each learner learns in a particular way. Inclusive teaching is about helping all learners to optimise their own individual learning and to get the most from their learning journeys.

In order to do this we need to ensure our colleges respect and value all learners and are places where they can feel safe and free to voice their own opinions. Many colleges will encourage their learners to become active citizens and to be involved in the decision-making processes that exist. They can do this by being a student representative, taking part in student forums, student union activities, community work, etc.

When everyone is able to be actively involved in the community then the community becomes truly inclusive.

CASE STUDY

There is nothing special about the tutor group I have chosen to focus on except for the students themselves. You could walk into any college and encounter a similar group. I have chosen them from all the other groups I have taught because I liked them very much and grew to understand with their help that inclusion is not just a concept to try to apply. It is a fact of life that we do anyway, completely instinctively, in our everyday teaching.

Differentiation means recognising that each learner in the class differs in many ways. Once this has been recognised it is just a matter of planning each teaching and learning session so that, despite these differences, all can find a way of learning and ultimately achieve their goals.

When you look at the individual profiles of just six of the students in this class you begin to see and to understand the extent and complexity of each student's previous personal and educational experiences that have led to this point in their learning journey. These students are studying for a BTEC National Certificate in Travel & Tourism (level 3) and are completing the second and final year. The course is assessed by course work and is the equivalent to two A levels.

The teaching team are dedicated Travel & Tourism specialists with a wealth of industrial and teaching experience. Their personal tutor had this to say about her group: 'I am incredibly proud of their achievements. Many of this group would not have made it this far without their individual determination to succeed, in spite of external factors, and the support they give each other and receive from the staff at the college. Some of these students were let down by education and society in the past and have re-engaged and gone from strength to strength in their learning on this course.'

The fact that these students have found themselves in the same class at the same time is a tribute to the inclusive learning agenda, but it goes to show that if there is this much variety in the needs and expectations of students in one random group in one college, then most teachers and educators will be experiencing the same eclectic mix of learners and will be differentiating and adapting to their needs without the need for a 'theory' or a training course. It is in the soul of all 'good' teachers to do this, because it is impossible to deliver a good lesson without it.

Student A – Sarah – Age 29
Sarah is a mature student who has two children and has returned to education in order to improve her chances in life and to gain employment in the travel industry locally. She likes the fact that lessons are relaxed and tutors are helpful. Sarah has received help from the learner-support fund to assist with trips and visits and a crèche place for her son.

Student B – Helen – Age 33
Helen is a single parent to two children and feels that the course has helped her become more positive and confident about starting a career in Travel & Tourism. Helen has benefited from the learner-support fund to help towards her course fees and a crèche place for her daughter. Helen has enjoyed coming to college and has made some lovely friends. Her tutor has been particularly helpful in supporting her and encouraging her to stay on the course, even when things have been difficult at home.

Student C – Paul – Age 19
Paul is partially sighted and started at the college when he left school at 16. He started on the level 1 – Introductory Diploma in Travel & Tourism and has progressed through dogged determination via the level 2 – First Diploma in Travel & Tourism to the course he is on now. Paul has a one-to-one support worker in all his lessons and has been provided with a laptop to help him with his work. He has enjoyed his four years at the college, particularly the trips and residentials, and feels he is more confident, wise and realistic now. He would like to work as a guide/support worker on holidays for partially sighted people when he finishes the course.

Student D – Jenni – Age 18

Jenni was a high achiever at school and came straight on to the level 3 programme. Jenni is very quiet and hard working and enjoys the course and the friends she has made. She received an Education Maintenance Allowance (EMA) and was given a free place on residential last year for being the hardest working student in the department. Jenni intends to go to university when she finishes the course.

Student E – Simon – Age 18

Simon has semantic pragmatic disorder, which is a term used for people who show autistic spectrum tendencies and specific language difficulties that cause complex communication problems. Simon is taking the course over three years not two, to allow him to work at his own pace and to cope with the difficulties he encounters on a day-to-day basis. He is enjoying the course and is making outstanding progress. His confidence and organisational skills are improving and he is benefiting from one-to-one support in his lessons. Simon would like to work in a passenger transport agency when he leaves the programme.

Student F – Sima – Age 18

Sima came on to the course directly from school and was in a group with two other Asian girls and three Asian boys. She was lively and contributed well to the course. Due to personal difficulties Sima had to drop out of her second year and has re-started this year with a different cohort. Unfortunately, she is the only Asian in the class. However, this does not deter her and she is making friends and growing in confidence. She would like to go to university when she leaves and particularly values the support from her tutor and the financial support she gets via the EMA.

From the case study I have identified the following themes that support the inclusion of learners in FE and their ability to learn and succeed in their education.

Support

Support for learners can be broken down into three further sections: learner support; financial support; and tutorial support.

Student C – Phil and student E – Simon have one-to-one support in the classroom in order to enable them to participate in the learning and this support has also been available on residential visits and trips ensuring they are fully able to participate in the vocational experience the courses offer. This support is not about doing the work for the students but about helping them to develop their own skills and abilities.

All of the students benefit from financial support. This varies from free crèche places, help towards the cost of residentials to the EMA. The EMA is a government initiative that allows young people from low income families to claim up to £30 per week towards the costs incurred in attending college. The rationale for this is to break the link between socio-economic status, educational achievement and future employability. 'I would not be able to attend college without the EMA as my family would not be able to give me money to come to college.' Student D – Jenni. (Note: at the time of writing there are proposals to withdraw the EMA from all learners.)

The provision of free crèche places for adults has enabled mature women returners to come back to education and to provide a better life for their families. 'The crèche has been a lifesaver for me as it means I can study and know my daughter is close by and being looked after. I would never have come to college if it had not been there.' Student B – Helen.

Tutorial support is essential and is highly valued by all learners. 'My tutor has been particularly helpful in supporting me and encouraging me to stay on the course even when things have been difficult at home.' Student B – Helen.

Tutors in FE develop strong personal relationships with their tutor groups and provide one-to-one support and group tutorials covering issues such as citizenship, being healthy and achieving economic well-being. This role is designed to support and encourage learners to maximise their potential and become self-sufficient workers who contribute to society. By adopting a humanistic approach where tutors respect their learners, empathise with them and show themselves to be genuine, a positive relationship can be built with learners on an individualised basis.

The role of the personal tutor and the resources and training allocated to this role determine the success not just of the role but of the students within that tutor group. Good tutors will retain and motivate their students and encourage them to succeed.

Curriculum

Successful organisations are part of the wider social context they represent and they will have built a relationship with that community which allows them to know how to meet their present and future education needs.

The curriculum provision of an organisation is a measure of that institution's close relationship with the community it serves and its diverse population. Curriculum in lifelong learning is designed to meet the needs of all learners and to be responsive to the needs of society and employers. Learners can access a wide and diverse curriculum and, depending on their entry qualifications, can study from entry level 1 to level 5 across all vocational areas.

In specific situations, the curriculum can be adapted to meet the learning needs of certain learners. In the case of student E – Simon, the two-year BTEC programme he chose to study was spread over three years to enable him to work at his own pace and to achieve the full qualification. This flexibility is essential in providing inclusive learning opportunities.

Ethos and environment

The ethos and environment in lifelong learning is fundamental to its success in achieving inclusive learning and to recruiting learners from hard-to-reach minority groups. Colleges are wholly dependent on recruitment, retention and achievement for their funding, and success is judged by the extent to which they retain the learners they recruit and the extent to which those learners achieve their learning outcomes. The ethos and environment are significant in attracting learners and ensuring they enjoy the experience.

The Every Child Matters (ECM) agenda underpins the ethos and environment in colleges by focusing on four key themes: being healthy and staying safe; enjoying and achieving; making a positive contribution; and economic well-being.

This approach considers the whole experience of the student – a holistic approach – and the need to provide practical and emotional support to enable them to complete and succeed in their learning journey in a responsive and supportive learning environment.

Resources

Physical and human resources are required to ensure a fully inclusive experience for learners. It is essential that the initial feeling for all students when entering a college and using the facilities is welcoming. If this does not happen for any reason, students feel isolated and segregated. The chance of colleges turning this into a positive, inclusive experience will be lost.

The provision of high-quality resources, including buildings, is essential to meet the needs of learners. By providing learning-support assistants, student-support services, careers advice, crèches, ICT (including the provision of laptops and specialist equipment) we are better placed to enable students to succeed.

The cost of providing these resources is mitigated by the financial benefits gained by the successful achievement of the learners. 'My laptop helps me to fit in in class, I can have the work in a font I can see without needing to have special equipment or make a fuss!' Student C – Paul.

Participation

'The best bit of the course is the residentials and trips I have been able to go on. My support worker comes as well and helps me to see everything. The other students are great; they all help me and make sure I am treated the same.' Student C – Paul.

Being able to fully participate in the learning programme and the day-to-day life of the college is essential to ensure all learners can be involved and all voices are heard. *Learning is a weapon against poverty. It is the route to participation and active citizenship* (Kennedy, 1997, page 4).

It is the provision of opportunities to participate, and the provision of the resources and materials to support the learners in that participation, that will address the negative experiences of disadvantaged individuals and communities.

PRACTICAL TASK PRACTICAL TASK **PRACTICAL TASK** PRACTICAL TASK **PRACTICAL TASK**

Consider one of the groups you teach and identify the range of students. What support do they receive and how does it help them?

In the lifelong learning sector inclusion can also apply to efforts to recruit those usually under-represented: single parents; long-term unemployed; immigrant communities; older learners; learners with disabilities; learners with specific needs; and those not in education, employment or training (NEETs).

One impact of these policies and practices is the need to provide teaching and learning activities for a wider range of students in any one session.

The design and delivery of learning programmes must include extra help for people who have not previously succeeded.

(Kennedy, 1997, page 10)

Everyone who can benefit from further education should be able to participate. We must ensure that all who want further education can be welcomed on terms they can accept.

(FEFC, 1996)

A fully inclusive college enrols and supports learners effectively, identifies individual learning requirements and makes sure these requirements are met. It matches the learning environment to the student, rather than expecting the student to fit in to whatever happens to be available.

We can see from the case study that in the college investigated, the individual needs of the learners are being addressed and the curriculum adapted or supported to enable them to succeed. A wide range of learners are being recruited on to programmes, with the only proviso being they have the correct academic entry criteria for each level of study. All of this is supported by, and contributes to, the culture and ethos of the college in question.

A SUMMARY OF **KEY POINTS**

In this chapter we have:
> **explored themes of culture, ethos and values in education;**
> **discussed the role of communication in creating a culture;**
> **considered the role of inclusion and differentiation;**
> **identified strategies that will enable you to understand the culture and support learners in your organisation.**

REFERENCES REFERENCES REFERENCES REFERENCES REFERENCES REFERENCES

FEFC (1996) *Inclusive Learning: Report of the Learning Difficulties and/or Disabilities Committee.* London: HMSO.

Kennedy, H (1997) *Learning Works: Widening Participation in Further Education.* Coventry: FEFC.

Lumby, J (2001) *Managing Further Education: Learning Enterprise.* London: Paul Chapman Publishing.

Nagel, G (1998) *The Tao of Teaching.* New York: Plume.

FURTHER READING FURTHER READING FURTHER READING FURTHER READING

You might like to read the following books:

Bush, T and Middlewich, D (2005) *Leading and Managing People in Education.* London: Sage.
This book focuses on leading and managing people within the workplace. It provides an interesting insight into the role of managers in creating culture and managing change.

Busher, H (2006) *Understanding Educational Leadership – People, Power and Culture.* Maidenhead: Open University Press.
  This book is good because it focuses on specific issues that affect culture in educational contexts. This is particularly helpful for people new to management.

Also:

Fawbert, F (2008) *Teaching in Post-Compulsory Education: Skills, Standards and Lifelong Learning.* London: Continuum.

Lea, J, Hayes, D, Armitage, A, Lomas, L and Markless, S (2003) *Working in Post-Compulsory Education.* Maidenhead: Open University Press.

Wallace, S (2007) *Teaching, Tutoring and Training in the Lifelong Learning Sector* (3rd ed). Exeter: Learning Matters.

Websites

Semantic pragmatic support group www.spdsupport.org.uk

8
Professionalism and accountability

This chapter is designed to:

- provide you with a clear understanding of professionalism in the lifelong learning sector;
- outline issues of accountability and how they affect you as a teacher;
- consider the role of the Institute for Learning (IfL) and qualifications designed to professionalise the industry;
- focus on how you can be professional and maintain your licence to practise;
- discuss how safeguarding and other issues affect you in your role.

It addresses the following Professional Standards for QTLS:

AS 4 Reflection and evaluation of their own practice and their continuing professional development as teachers.

AS 6 The application of agreed codes of practice and the maintenance of a safe environment.

It also addresses the Level 5 DTTLS module: Continuing personal and professional development.

Introduction

The wise teacher is not collecting a string of successes. The teacher is helping others to find their own success. There is plenty to go around. Sharing success with others is very successful.
The single principle behind all creation teaches us that true benefit blesses everyone and diminishes no one.
The wise teacher knows that the reward for doing the work arises naturally out of the work.
(Adapted from Heider, 1985, page 161)

We all remember the teachers who inspired us and helped us to succeed. They were responsible for sparking an interest in education, raising our aspirations and setting us up for our future careers. These teachers were professional practitioners who took their roles seriously and helped and guided us on our way.

So, how do we define professionalism in the context of the lifelong learning sector?

PRACTICAL TASK PRACTICAL TASK PRACTICAL TASK PRACTICAL TASK PRACTICAL TASK

List the behaviours that you think make a professional teacher.

Professionalism and accountability

Traditionally, the term 'professional' has been synonymous with, for example, doctors, lawyers and clergymen, and holds within its meaning an implication that it involves some sort of 'oath' to serve the common good. Society deems a profession such as this should be self-regulating and responsible for upholding its own values, practices and behaviours via its own professional code of conduct.

In recent history teaching has come to be viewed as a profession and, as such, has developed its own professional values and behaviours. It is, however, also heavily monitored and controlled by government and its inspection regimes. Avis (2010, page 6) contradicts this by saying that *the state views the FE teacher in particular as a service provider, at the behest of the market, one who will acquire earned autonomy as a 'trusted servant' of the state*, rather than as a professional in their own right.

When attempting to define professionalism as it relates to teachers in the lifelong learning sector in particular, we need to look at the three concepts of:

* professional knowledge;
* autonomy;
* responsibility.

It is because professionals face complex and unpredictable situations that they need a specialist body of knowledge; if they are able to apply that knowledge, it is argued that they need the autonomy to make their own judgements. Given that they have autonomy, it is essential that they act with responsibility – collectively they need to develop professional values.

(Furlong et al., 2000, page 5, cited in Robson, 2006, page 11)

We might say then that the professional teacher upholds the values and behaviours of the 'profession', working autonomously for the good of their students and the benefit of society as a whole.

They exhibit a level of behaviour and performance that includes not only the high quality of their teaching, but their ability to adhere to a code of practice and given set of values. One thing that marks us out as teachers in the lifelong learning sector is our daily contact with young people and vulnerable adults and the consequent necessity to act as a positive role model and as a supportive professional, using criticism only as a tool for positive reinforcement.

The term 'accountability' means the public's holding to account of professionals for their behaviour, results and performance. They answer to the organisation, the government, to the students they teach and their parents. The current legislative climate in which schools and colleges can be sued as a result of their failing to meet the needs of students and staff means that issues of accountability are at the forefront of most organisations' policies and practices.

As professional teachers we conform to the codes of practice of our profession and we are held accountable for any breaches in meeting those standards.

PRACTICAL TASK PRACTICAL TASK **PRACTICAL TASK** PRACTICAL TASK **PRACTICAL TASK**

Find out if your organisation has a code of practice – what does it include?

Professionalism in the lifelong learning sector

In 2004, the government proposed reforms to the initial teacher training procedure for teachers entering into the lifelong learning sector. The government stated its commitment to providing a well-qualified and professional workforce for the sector and introduced a set of professional standards. These standards were developed by Lifelong Learning UK (LLUK), which is the sector skills council responsible for the professional development of those working in the sector.

The new standards were introduced in the White Paper *Raising Skills, Improving Life Chances* (DfES, 2006). The following is an extract from the professional standards:

> *The professional standards for teachers, tutors and trainers in the lifelong learning sector describe, in generic terms, the skills, knowledge and attributes required of those who perform the wide variety of teaching and training roles undertaken within the sector with learners and employers.*

> *Not all standards will necessarily relate to all teaching roles. Rather they supply the basis for the development of contextualised role specifications and units of assessment, which provide benchmarks for performances in practice of the variety of roles performed by teachers, trainers, tutors and lecturers within the lifelong learning sector. Together, these will identify the components of: the initial teaching award (Passport); qualifications leading to Qualified Teacher, Learning and Skills (QTLS) status; and other intermediate and advanced teaching qualifications.*

> *These developments will be complemented by a new Continuing Professional Development (CPD) expectation of teachers and trainers of, at the very least, 30 hours per year.*

> *Teachers in the lifelong learning sector value all learners individually and equally.*

> *They are committed to lifelong learning and professional development and strive for continuous improvement through reflective practice. The key purpose of the teacher is to create effective and stimulating opportunities for learning through high quality teaching that enables the development and progression of all learners.*

> *These are the overarching professional standards for all those who teach in the lifelong learning sector.*

> *Domain A. Professional values and practice.*
> *Domain B. Learning and teaching.*
> *Domain C. Specialist learning and teaching.*
> *Domain D. Planning for learning.*
> *Domain E. Assessment for learning.*
> *Domain F. Access and progression.*

> (*New Professional Standards for Teachers, Tutors and Trainers in the Lifelong Learning Sector*, LLUK, 2006)

Alongside this came the introduction of the Institute for Learning (IfL) in 2002 as the professional body for teachers in the lifelong learning sector. All teachers in the sector now have to register with the IfL and remain in good standing through CPD. This applies to existing teachers and those new to teaching in the sector.

The IfL has introduced a code of professional practice, which is based on six core principles or behaviours:

1. Integrity
2. Respect
3. Care
4. Practice
5. Disclosure
6. Responsibility.

1 Professional integrity
You are expected to use reasonable professional judgement when discharging differing responsibilities and obligations to learners, colleagues, institutions and the wider profession. You are also expected to uphold the reputation of the profession by never unjustly or knowingly damaging the professional reputation of another or furthering your own position unfairly at the expense of another.

2 Respect
You must respect the rights of learners and colleagues in accordance with relevant legislation and organisation requirements and also act in a manner which recognises diversity as an asset and does not discriminate in respect of race, gender, disability and/or learning difficulty, age, sexual orientation or religion and belief.

3 Reasonable care
Members will take reasonable care to ensure the safety and welfare of learners and comply with relevant statutory provisions to support their well-being and development.

4 Professional practice
Members will provide evidence to the Institute that they have complied with the current Institute CPD policy and guidelines.

5 Criminal offence disclosure
Any member shall notify the Institute as soon as practicable after cautioning or conviction for a criminal offence. The Institute reserves the right to act on such information through its disciplinary process.

6 Responsibility to the Institute
The members shall at all times act in accordance with the Institute's conditions of membership, which will be subject to change from time to time.

There are four sanctions which can be applied to members who breach the Code of Professional Practice:

- A reprimand.
- A Conditional Registration Order.
- A Suspension Order.
- An Expulsion Order.

The nature of the sanction imposed will depend upon the circumstances of the case.

What does this mean in practice?

1. Valuing all learners and giving them all the same opportunities
    As teachers we need to make sure we take into account the diverse needs of all of the learners in our groups and to ensure we treat them all fairly. We need to respect their beliefs and behaviours, their age, race, gender, disability and sexual orientation. We need to celebrate difference and embrace it so that all students feel at home in the learning environment and that the learning outcomes are achieved by all.

    Sometimes it is necessary to treat people differently in order to offer them the same opportunities. For example, it is good practice to offer a student who is a second language speaker extra support in ESOL (English as a second language), in order to help them achieve the same outcomes as the other learners on the programme.

2. Delivering high quality lessons
    As discussed in Chapter 2, delivering high quality lessons is imperative and a key part of the role of the professional teacher. Taking the time to plan and prepare interesting and diverse lessons that meet the needs of all learners is a key indicator of our ability to perform at the highest professional standards.

3. Being well prepared and well resourced
    Most organisations will have a set requirement with regard to lesson plans and schemes of work. It is your professional duty to produce these in the format required in as much detail as you can. You are also required to plan your lessons and prepare the resources required to deliver them. These resources should meet the required format of the organisation and be in a sans serif font at least size 12 with 1.5 line spacing and be on cream paper to meet the needs of dyslexic learners.

4. Being early to class and finishing on time
    Again, organisations will have their own guidelines but it customary to arrive at lessons before the students and to set up the room appropriately. Greeting the students as they enter the classroom is a good way of developing positive relationships and of engaging with them as individuals.

    Finishing lessons on time is a requirement and it is unprofessional to let students leave early unless it is in order for them to get to their next lesson on time. You are also in breach of your duty of care if you leave students unsupervised for any part of the lesson for which you are responsible.

5. Dressing and behaving appropriately
    As professionals it is important to dress and behave appropriately with students.

    Your organisation will have guidelines on suitable dress, but it is safe to say that smart/smart casual is appropriate. Avoid low-cut tops, short skirts, jeans and trainers. It is important that students perceive you as 'the teacher' and the image you portray is part of this.

    Appropriate behaviour includes your language, body language and relationships with students. Avoid swearing, shouting, bullying language, over-familiar language, sexual innuendo and sharing too much personal information. Make sure you avoid physical contact with students and that your body language is respectful and positive.

Close relationships with students are unprofessional and in many cases will result in disciplinary action by your employer. Even becoming friends outside of the classroom can lead to difficult situations and accusations of unprofessional behaviour.

6. Respecting the opinions of others
    Showing respect for others in all aspects of our work is essential. We need to work at developing professional relationships with our colleagues, line managers and the management and to show respect and professionalism in our working practices.

    This respect must be obvious to our students and it is imperative that we never disparage another member of staff in front of students by questioning their behaviour or decisions.

7. Meeting all deadlines
    As professional teachers we will be given a variety of deadlines to meet. It is essential that we do our utmost to meet these deadlines, particularly those that relate to the assessment of student work and meeting awarding body requirements.

8. Maintaining accurate records
    You have a legal obligation to maintain appropriate records which are accurate, detailed and legible. They must be completed on time and failure to do so can result in disciplinary action.

9. Ensuring you meet your duty-of-care obligations
    Under safeguarding legislation we have a duty of care to our young people and vulnerable adults. We must report to the designated person any instances of suspected abuse or neglect of anyone in our care. Even though many of our students will be over 18 they are still classified as vulnerable adults in our care and, as such, we must be responsible for their safety. This means their emotional and psychological safety as well as physical safety.

10. Full disclosure
    You must ensure that you have a full CRB check and that you disclose immediately any changes that occur to your status.

REFLECTIVE TASK

Consider what you would do in the following situations.

1. You are a new member of staff aged 27 and you have two young daughters who are in the college crèche. It is your elder daughter's 4th birthday and her best friends are the children of people who are in your class. She wants to invite them to her birthday party. What do you do?

2. You live in a small town and have just started to teach at the local college. There is only one nightclub in the town and you are used to going there with your friends on a Friday night. You arrive at the club to find that there are a group of your students in the bar. They are all under age. What do you do?

3. You have a child who attends the same college that you teach at. He is not studying in your subject area but you know the staff who teach him. He has a friend who often visits your home who also goes to the college. You become aware that this friend is being badly treated at home by his father. What do you do?

[The suggested answers to these questions are at the end of the chapter.]

TOP **TIPS** TOP TIPS TOP TIPS TOP TIPS **TOP TIPS** TOP TIPS TOP TIPS TOP TIPS

Top tips for being a professional teacher

- Be friendly but not friends.
- Be concerned but not intrusive.
- Be aware but not too knowing.
- Be strong but not too hard.
- Be fair but not indecisive.
- Be organised but not obsessive.
- Be structured but not inflexible.
- Be prepared to take action but not too quick to take action.
- Be clear about consequences but not rigid.
- Be yourself but do not share too much of yourself.

Professional qualifications to teach in the lifelong learning sector

As mentioned earlier, in 2004 the government introduced a range of new teaching qualifications designed to professionalise the sector and to take into account the diversity and variety of roles that teaching staff undertake.

We are going to deal in outline with the main qualifications. These qualifications are:

- **Preparing to Teach in the Lifelong Learning Sector** (PTLLS);
- **Certificate in Teaching in the Lifelong Learning Sector** (CTLLS);
- **Diploma in Teaching in the Lifelong Learning Sector** (DTLLS);
- **Certificate in Education/Certificate in Higher Education** (Cert Ed/Cert HE);
- **Professional Graduate Certificate in Education** (PGCE);
- **Certificate in Assessing Candidates Using a Range of Methods (A1– Vocational Assessor Award)**;
- **Conduct Internal Quality Assurance of the Assessment Process (V1 – Vocational Internal Verifiers Award)**.

PTLLS

This award is available at two levels:

- Level 3 Award in Preparing to Teach in the Lifelong Learning Sector (PTLLS).
- Level 4 Award in Preparing to Teach in the Lifelong Learning Sector (PTLLS).

This comprises one 6-credit unit entitled 'Preparing to Teach in the Lifelong Learning Sector'. This qualification provides a basic minimum standard for all those entering the profession from September 2007.

The qualification involves:

- initial assessment of literacy, numeracy and ICT needs, and planning to address these;
- in-service, pre-service or pre-employment – intended as precursor to teaching;

- observed practice (can be micro teaching);
- mentoring support.

It confers threshold status to teach.

It will be expected that someone enrolling on an initial award will normally possess at least a minimum level 3 qualification in their own area of specialism.

CTLLS

This qualification will be taken by teachers in an associate teacher role. The role of the associate teacher is defined in the Further Education Teachers' Qualifications (England) Regulations (LLUK, 2007):

> *'Associate teaching role' means a teaching role that carries significantly less than the full range of teaching responsibilities ordinarily carried out in a full teaching role (whether on a full-time, part-time, fractional, fixed term, temporary or agency basis) and does not require the teacher to demonstrate an extensive range of knowledge, understanding and application of curriculum development, curriculum innovation or curriculum delivery strategies.*

This certificate is available at two levels:

- Level 3 Certificate in Teaching in the Lifelong Learning Sector.
- Level 4 Certificate in Teaching in the Lifelong Learning Sector.

Units of assessment for the Level 3 Certificate in Teaching in the Lifelong Learning Sector:

Mandatory units

Level 3.	6 credits.	Preparing to teach in the lifelong learning sector.
Level 3.	9 credits.	Planning and enabling learning.
Level 3.	3 credits.	Principles and practice of assessment.

Optional units
To the value of at least 6 credits at a minimum of level 3.

Units of assessment for the Level 4 Certificate in Teaching in the Lifelong Learning Sector

Mandatory units

Level 4.	6 credits.	Preparing to teach in the lifelong learning sector.
Level 4.	9 credits.	Planning and enabling learning.
Level 4.	3 credits.	Principles and practice of assessment.

Optional units
A minimum of 6 credits at level 3 or 4.

DTLLS

This will be taken by teachers in a full teacher role. This role is defined in the Further Education Teachers' Qualifications (England) Regulations (LLUK, 2007):

'Full teaching role' means a teaching role that carries the full range of teaching responsibilities (whether on a full-time, part-time, fractional, fixed term, temporary or agency basis) and requires the teacher to demonstrate an extensive range of knowledge, understanding and application of curriculum development, curriculum innovation or curriculum delivery strategies.

Units of assessment for the Level 5 Diploma in Teaching in the Lifelong Learning Sector

Part One

Mandatory units

Level 4.	6 credits.	Preparing to teach in the lifelong learning sector.
Level 4.	9 credits.	Planning and enabling learning.
Level 4.	15 credits.	Enabling learning and assessment.
Level 4.	15 credits.	Theories and principles for planning and enabling learning.

Optional units

To the value of **15** credits at a minimum of level 4.

Part Two

Mandatory units

Level 5.	15 credits.	Continuing personal and professional development.
Level 5.	15 credits.	Curriculum design for inclusive practice.
Level 5.	15 credits.	Wider professional practice.

Optional units

A minimum of 15 credits at level 5.

Teaching practice

There must be a minimum of 150 hours of teaching practice.

Cert Ed/Cert HE

These programmes are offered by universities as full- or part-time courses to people who are either already working in, or want to work in, the lifelong learning sector.

These are level 5 qualifications that incorporate the professional standards for teachers, tutors and trainers in the lifelong learning sector and incorporate the PTLLS, CTLLS and DTLLS qualifications. In most cases they are approved by Standards Verification UK, the endorsing body of LLUK, and enable successful trainees to graduate and have eligibility for QTLS.

The content of these programmes varies from institution to institution but will always include 150 hours of teaching practice and a minimum of eight observed teaching sessions.

PGCE

These programmes are offered by universities as full- or part-time courses to people who are either already working in, or want to work in, the lifelong learning sector and who are graduates in their specialist areas.

These are level 6 qualifications that incorporate the professional standards for teachers, tutors and trainers in the lifelong learning sector and incorporate the PTLLS, CTLLS and DTLLS qualifications. In most cases they are approved by SVUK (the awarding body for PTLLS, CTLLS and DTLLS) and enable successful trainees to graduate and have eligibility for QTLS.

The content of these programmes varies from institution to institution but will always include 150 hours of teaching practice and a minimum of eight observed teaching sessions.

These days, most universities offer the opportunity for you to complete up to 60 credits at level 7 to enable you to achieve a PGCE and progress on to a Masters programme.

A1 – Vocational Assessor Award

The A1 award is designed to offer those individuals who are, or will be, concerned with assessing learners taking NVQs. It is a programme of training in skills, techniques and principles of assessing competency using a variety of assessment methods.

This is not a qualification that replaces a teaching award but it is an extra qualification needed to enable you to assess NVQ programmes. It is a level 3 qualification and consists of a portfolio of evidence submitted to the awarding body for assessment.

V1 – Vocational Internal Verifiers Award

The V1 award is a nationally recognised and widely used competence-based programme that enables individuals to conduct internal quality assurance checks of the assessment process for NVQ programmes.

This qualification follows the A1 award and is essential to those who verify the work of other assessors in vocational settings.

All of these qualifications are designed to make sure teachers working in the sector are professionally qualified and meet rigorous standards in their planning, delivery and assessment of the students in their organisations. However, this is not the end of the story. Once employed in the sector you must adhere to both the IfL code of conduct and that of your organisation. But, most importantly, you must become 'professional' in your behaviour and accountable for your actions. Every part of your lives will be affected by this commitment to being a professional teacher and you will be judged and held accountable for any failings.

From a personal point of view you need to consider things such as:

● social networking sites – how much personal information is it professional for you to share?
● socialising – what pubs and clubs can you go to in order to avoid students?
● behaviour likely to attract attention – e.g. drunk and disorderly behaviour that might be observed or reported back to students and colleagues. Is this unprofessional?
● other employment – even if you work part-time, any other employment you have will lay you open to scrutiny. If you work in a bar at the weekends are you likely to be put in difficult situations?
● eating out – most students have part-time jobs and you will often come across them as waiting staff in restaurants. How do you deal with this? What about tipping?

A colleague tells the following story: *As a newly qualified teacher and a young single mother I found it difficult to do my shopping at my local supermarket as a number of my students worked there and I felt they were watching what I bought. I was embarrassed by my choice of value products and cheap alcohol. I found myself travelling to another town in order to shop in privacy!*

Another colleague tells of how they went to a local hotel for a weekend spa break and ordered breakfast in bed only to have it delivered the next morning by a student in her A level Law class!

As you can see, the whole area is fraught with difficult situations just waiting to catch us out and we need to keep our wits about us in order to maintain our professionalism and reputation.

PRACTICAL TASK PRACTICAL TASK **PRACTICAL TASK** PRACTICAL TASK **PRACTICAL TASK**

Consider potential situations that could affect you and come up with a plan to minimise their impact.

Safeguarding young people and vulnerable adults

Education providers in the lifelong learning and skills sector have responsibilities to ensure the safety of young people and those adults deemed 'vulnerable'. A vulnerable adult is defined as a person *who is or may be in need of community care services by reason of mental or other disability, age or illness; and who is or may be unable to take care of him or herself, or unable to protect him or herself against significant harm or exploitation* (Department of Health, 2000).

In the context of our role, all of our adult learners can be classified as 'vulnerable' in the sense that they are under our influence and the influence of their peers and therefore may be unable to protect themselves against exploitation, bullying and being unduly influenced to behave in a certain way. Fortunately, cases of abuse in education and training provision are rare. However, the reporting, to trusted staff, of abuse that occurs outside the training and learning environment, is not uncommon. Education and training providers need to be prepared to deal with all aspects of creating a safer environment.

Creating a 'safer' learning environment that promotes well-being and security is essential for all learners and all staff. While it is important to recognise that certain groups of people are legally identified as vulnerable, and to have relevant policies, procedures and practices in place, it is better to have fully inclusive and integrated 'safer' practices that apply to all staff and learners. This creates a safer environment for all.

There are many examples of situations where young people and vulnerable adults have been let down by the education system and have suffered harm as a result. Your professional duty is to follow the procedures that exist in your organisation and to report any instances of neglect, abuse, bullying, etc. to the designated safeguarding officer for appropriate action to be taken.

9
Working in teams

This chapter is designed to:

- provide you with a clear understanding of the concept of quality assurance and quality improvement within a collaborative approach to the sector;
- establish some appreciation of key social and psychological factors that shape how we work with others;
- consider the impact of working as an effective team member.

It addresses the following Professional Standards for QTLS:

AS 5 Collaboration with other individuals, groups and/or organisations with a legitimate interest in the progress and development of learners.

AK 5.1 Ways to communicate and collaborate with colleagues and/or others to enhance learners' experience.

DS 3 Evaluation of own effectiveness in planning learning.

DK 3.2 Ways to evaluate own role and performance as a member of a team in planning learning.

ES 5 Working within the systems and quality requirements of the organisation in relation to assessment and monitoring of learner progress.

EK 5.3 The necessary/appropriate assessment information to communicate to others who have a legitimate interest in learner achievement.

FS 4 A multi-agency approach to supporting development and progression opportunities for learners.

FK 4.2 Processes for liaison with colleagues and other professionals to provide effective guidance and support for learners.

Introduction – working effectively in teams

> *There may be no 'I' in team, but there's a 'ME' if you look hard enough.*
> (Attributed to the character David Brent in *The Office* but used by many others)

> *If I could solve all the problems myself, I would.*
> (Thomas Edison, on being asked why he had 21 assistants)

The above quotations offer two approaches to the elusive nature of the social conundrum that can be called teamwork. One aspect of quality that needs to be recognised and understood, particularly by new entrants to the sector, is the importance of effective teamwork in executing the role for which they have been trained. Maybe it's because there is a predominant focus on 'the' teacher, the lone expert bravely entering the lion's den of a classroom, but it's my experience that teachers are often guilty of forgetting they are only one part of a much bigger organisation.

CASE STUDY

Some years ago I was personal tutor to a group of students, one of whom was a 22-year-old returner to education. She had a two-year-old daughter and had a history of personal issues. She was attempting to change her life and provide a secure upbringing for her daughter, having recently left her drug-dealing boyfriend who was the father of the child.

With a history of domestic abuse at his hands she was living in fear of further violence. She phoned me one evening in desperation, saying he was trying to break in to the house and the police were unable to attend for another two hours due to a major incident. I could hear the child crying and the door being attacked.

This was a very difficult situation as I felt it was inappropriate to intervene on my own, but felt responsible for her and her daughter's safety. I contacted my line manager and with him and a couple of other staff we went to the house and removed the student and child to a women's refuge in a local town.

She was then moved to another refuge 60 miles away and transferred to another college to complete her studies.

Although in this situation we were unable to follow the exact procedures in place at the college, we acted in a professional way and were able to safeguard the student and her child, and ensure they were able to make a new start away from the violence.

REFLECTIVE TASK

Reflect on this example and how you would act in a similar situation.

CASE STUDY
Chris Horne

After two years of studying for my Cert Ed I now found myself wanting more from my time at college.

I was quite fortunate to get some good grades from my lesson observations with my tutor and my mentor, which was when it was put to me by my Cert Ed tutor to look more closely into becoming a Teaching & Learning Coach (TLC).

My line manager had been asking for a TLC for quite a while, so when I went to him and asked could he put my name forward he was overjoyed to say the least.

After an application and an interview with the Head of Quality at college, they accepted me as a TLC for my department.

Wow. Here I was, just qualified, full of new ideas and straight from Cert Ed, ready to help my fellow colleagues. At first I was giving all my resources to all the staff and saying 'Try this', however, now I seem to be listening to more of their questions on *how* to teach rather than *what* to teach.

I have been to several staff development days for TLCs and found that this is what we need to do, to encourage our colleagues to develop their own professionalism and resources. Being the TLC for my department has certainly helped me to open up to a person's potential and to help them with different ideas and ways of engaging the students, after all they are the pivotal ones in the classroom not the lecturer (just ask Ofsted).

It was once said to me that 'moving towards a solution is better than moving away from a problem', this is quite true when it comes to coaching people.

I have recently been working with a member of staff who has been working hard at his teaching but is new to teaching and is finding it difficult to differentiate his questioning to the students. After a little guidance and lots of listening from me, he has improved his questioning technique and his observation grades have improved and has now had several observations graded at grade 2. His achievement was also my achievement and I feel that I have somehow put back into teaching something that I have taken out of my own learning.

After a recent Ofsted Monitoring visit, they remarked that a significant improvement in the teaching and learning has been reported, the achievement figures from our department have increased by 12%, this also goes hand in hand with the increase in retention of our students.

I feel that maybe this job was not all that bad after all. As a TLC I don't have all the answers; however I do have the time and professionalism to listen to a colleague; a problem shared is a problem halved.

We can see that this is an excellent example of professional teachers working together to support each other to benefit the students in the organisation.

A SUMMARY OF **KEY POINTS**

In this chapter we have:

> **considered the role of professionalism and accountability in the sector;**

> **discussed your role in being a professional teacher;**

> **considered qualifications, the code of conduct and the role of IfL;**

> **identified strategies that will enable you to become a 'professional' teacher.**

REFERENCES REFERENCES REFERENCES REFERENCES REFERENCES REFERENCES

Avis, J et al. (2010) *Teaching in Lifelong Learning.* Maidenhead: Open University Press.
DfES (2006) *Raising Skills, Improving Life Chances.* London: HMSO.
DH (2000) *Care Standards Act.* London: HMSO.
Heider, J (1985) *The Tao of Leadership.* Atlanta, GA: Humanics.
IFL (2008) *Code of Professional Practice.* www.ifl.ac.uk/membership/professionalstandards/code-of-professional-practice
LLUK (2007) *Guidance for Awarding Institutions on Teacher Roles and Initial Teaching Qualifications.* London: LLUK.
Robson, J (2006) *Teacher Professionalism in Further and Higher Education.* London: Routledge.

FURTHER READING FURTHER READING **FURTHER READING** FURTH

You might like to read the following books:

Tummons, J (2010) *Becoming a Professional Tutor in the Lifelong Learning Sector* Learning Matters.
This book focuses on professionalism, accountability and the practical aspec professional teacher in this very demanding sector.
Avis, J, Fisher, R and Thompson, R (2010) *Teaching in Lifelong Learning.* M University Press.
This book is good because it focuses on specific issues that occur in the lifelor and is full of useful hints and tips. This is particularly helpful for people new to good chapter on professionalism and its role in the sector.

Also:

Fairclough, M (2008) *Supporting Learners in the Lifelong Learning Sector.* Ma University Press.
Lawrence, D (2000) *Building Self-esteem With Adult Learners.* London: Paul Chapn
Steward, A (2009) *Continuing Your Professional Development in Lifelong Le* Continuum.

Websites

Institute for Learning www.ifl .ac.uk
Lifelong Learning UK www.lluk.org

Suggested answers to Reflective task, page 95:

1. You are a new member of staff aged 27 and you have two young daug in the college crèche. It is your elder daughter's fourth birthday and h are the children of people who are in your class. She wants to invit birthday party. What do you do?
   You have the party at a venue outside of your home and invite daughter wants to invite.

2. You live in a small town and have just started to teach at the local co only one nightclub in the town and you are used to going there with yo Friday night. You arrive at the club to find that there are a group of yo the bar. They are all under age. What do you do?

   Have a quiet word and let them know you have seen them. They shou very quickly. Choose another night club in a different area for future n

3. You have a child who attends the same college that you teach at. He is n your subject area but you know the staff who teach him. He has a frie visits your home who also goes to the college. You become aware that being badly treated at home by his father. What do you do?

   You need to pass the information to the staff who teach him and they w safeguarding procedures are followed.

One of the tensions within the whole domain of quality assurance and quality improvement is the extent to which you are seen to be personally responsible or collectively responsible. This individual versus collective responsibility impacts on the performance of individual teachers, curriculum or course teams, departments and whole colleges. What we intend to do in this chapter is to highlight some of those aspects where the individual and the collective come together, and to provide some insight into how you may fulfil an appropriate professional role within the wider parameters of a social organisation.

Organisational culture

Now it is very clear that, to some extent, the balance of individual and collective performance will reflect the nature of the organisational culture that is established – and indeed may have been established for quite some time. Moreover, this will affect both the explicit and implicit fulfilment of your role.

CASE STUDY
The story of the staffroom card-school

The following tale is offered honestly and seeks to impugn no one, however ....

In one college I worked at there was a very relaxed and sociable staffroom (this being before Ofsted, before LLUK, before the LSC). At lunchtime, a popular diversion was a game of Solo whist. Now you may not be a card player so you need to know that Solo whist can only be played by four people and there were at least seven keen players. As the game grew in popularity and in its competitiveness (a penny a point went into the end-of-term cake fund!) there was a noticeable increase in the desire to get a seat at the table. In those days there was a standard timetable with the end of morning lessons marked by the ringing of a bell right on 12.00 noon. While not a large college, in either physical size or student numbers, some classrooms were nearer to the staffroom and hence offered a greater chance of securing a seat at the table. Over a number of weeks it was evidently clear that finishing on time and arriving at the staffroom at two minutes past twelve was resulting in little or no chance to participate in the game. It became apparent that that the desire for a game of whist was overtaking some colleagues' desire to provide a full 60-minute lesson to their students because ... well, let's just say that one day, at five to twelve or thereabouts, seven participants were already in the staffroom. (You'll have to believe my protestation of innocence that I was the only one actually meant to be there as I was on administrative duties.)

Here is one aspect of group influence, of working with and around others, and the how such social behaviour contributes to the creation of an organisational culture, that is to say, a pervading sense of 'how things are done around here'. There was no discussion, certainly no remonstration, as all were equally guilty; there was some tacit justification, 'finishing early', 'good class', 'worked hard', and so on. It just became accepted that it was OK to finish a little early. (And indeed, in the right circumstances, both as a teacher and a manager I have used an 'early dart' as an appropriate reward to students and staff alike, but that''s another story.)

REFLECTIVE TASK

REFLECTIVE TASK

You are a trainee or perhaps a new member of staff. During the lunch break a student comes to the staffroom door, asks for a member of staff from your curriculum area but is told they are busy having lunch. You are not busy. Do you offer to deal with the enquiry instead?

You are a brave person if, in a relatively junior social position, you jump up and help, because possibly, as a result, you are going to make a colleague look less committed. I hope that jumping up and helping was at least your first thought and that you would be responsive to genuine student need. But there is a world between thought and action ...

This reflective task was posed because it mirrors the actuality of the staffroom culture at that time. The only phone in the staffroom was on a table next to the card school (see previous Case study). If it rang during the lunch break it was common to see colleagues pick up the phone and – without saying anything – replace it on the cradle. In a similar way, as in the reflective task above, any student calling at the staffroom door would be greeted – politely – with the information that 'we're having our lunch'.

Now, while I would not underestimate the genuine importance of work–life balance, and the necessity of staff getting a proper break, it never seemed right that this was the default position, as it were, that under no circumstances could a student have good enough reason to come to the staffroom at lunchtime.

The point here is that the stories above introduce something of the way in which culture and norms within an organisation can be developed. Here you see tacit acceptance of 'adjust-ment' to timetabled classes in order to enjoy company, conviviality and challenge away from the classroom; the perception that the phone would be bringing only 'more work'; the strongly held belief that the lunch break should indeed be a 'break' away from students.

In my own experience, as a new member of staff, I can well remember that there was a tangible sense of having to accept this behaviour and the climate in which it occurred, if only because it was what the majority of staff did. In his classic study of the behaviour within groups, Homans (1975) explained how social norms – shared expectations of acceptable behaviour within a group – are created. He described the subtle social interactions applied by men employed to install a new telephone system in a bank.

To secure conformity to unspoken and unwritten norms of behaviour, in terms of produc-tivity and work-rate, this 'bank-wiring group' would engage in banter and playful contact with newcomers to create the sense of what was acceptable. In his account, Homans substanti-ates the influence of the majority, an influence not always created by obviously direct language or behaviour. Indeed, much of it was coded and implicit, but nevertheless a real social force that shaped the attitude and behaviour of others, particularly those who were new to the group. When you join an organisation for the first time there will be these social forces – subtle and not so subtle – in action and you may, at times, without being able to fully articulate the problem, have a sense of tension between what you feel is appropriate and what seems to be common practice. You are experiencing the force of social norms, adjusting to ways of 'fitting in'.

The tension between the individual and the group to which they belong is significant within the context of organisational culture. Knights and Willmott (2007), among many others, suggest organisational culture is created by those assumptions, beliefs and values shared by the members of an organisation. And note that this is not the same as the organisation''s published 'Mission Statement' or declaration of 'Ethos and Values'. Now, this is a major field for the science of leadership and management and one for you to pursue with further reading if you are so minded. What is important in the context of this text and your professional setting is that organisational culture, while not explicitly recognised, is present in such a way as to be a determining factor upon both individual and group behaviours. As Schein notes, *Culture is an abstraction, yet the forces that are created in social and organisational situations are powerful* (2004, page 3).

One of the most powerful representations of this culture can be seen across the diverse work teams that are fundamental to the efficient running of a college or work-based learning provider. Estates, administration, finance, exams, technicians, learning support, catering, human resources, management, marketing – all necessary prerequisites for the most important, most prominent group, the teachers. They must be at the top of the tree, surely, because that is what the fundamental core of the business is, teaching. Isn't it?

Well arguably, it's not. The core business is learning and this is done by our learners, our students, our trainees, our customers if you must call them that. And if you have any doubt about the value and importance of the range of other roles, give it some thought:

REFLECTIVE TASK
BEELECLIAE 1V2K

In the middle of winter, just before the AS exam round, a major flu bug hits the town.

- Identify the non-teaching staff you could manage without if they were to phone in sick.
- Make a list of those non-teaching staff who you could not do without to get your job done.

Head of Human Resources, Head of Finance, even the Principal – would they be missed?

Caretaker, security, exams officer: who is going to let you into the building, into the room, into the safe to get the exam papers?

You are part of a multi-layered, social organisation and not everything is dependent on status and salary. Indeed, such is the necessity to work effectively with one's colleagues that it is a theme within the LLUK professional standards that is repeated several times.

It is acknowledged that we are only presenting a basic overview of organisational culture in recognising that our behaviour can be, and is, shaped by the actions of others not only at any given point of time but also by what behaviours have been seen and shared previously. We do, however, bring our own personal characteristics into any given culture and there has been some very effective work in scrutinising team performance by analysing the behaviours of those who constitute the group.

Effective groups

There is an overabundance of literature about teams and leadership: here we will provide a short introduction to two key models that will serve as a starting point for reflection, further reading and exploration.

Belbin's team roles model

Belbin (1981) identified nine team roles, which he categorised into three groups: action oriented; people oriented; and thought oriented. Each team role is associated with typical behavioural and interpersonal strengths.

Action oriented	People oriented	Thought oriented
Shapers	Co-ordinator	Plant
Implementer	Team worker	Monitor-evaluator
Completer-finisher	Resource investigator	Specialist

Table 9.1: Belbin's team roles

Action-oriented roles
● Shapers

Shapers are people who work in such a way as to challenge the team to improve. Usually extroverted people, they enjoy discussion, questioning, challenging, always looking for a new or better way. They will challenge complacency. They will often see obstacles as challenges and tend to have the courage to push on when others are reluctant.

They can be argumentative and they may offend other people's feelings by challenging and appearing to criticise their ideas and actions.

● Implementer

Implementers are the people who like to get things done. They are particularly good at turning ideas into action. The evidence suggests they are typically very well-organised people who work systematically and efficiently. They will be the people who leaders rely on to get the job done.

The downside is that they may be inflexible and somewhat resistant to change.

● Completer-finisher (CF)

Completer-finishers are the people who see that projects are completed and finished. They will look to make sure there have been no errors or omissions and they pay attention to details. A completer-finisher will be well aware of deadlines and will push the team to make sure the job is completed on time. Orderly, conscientious, and maybe even perfectionists, they may worry unnecessarily and find it hard to delegate.

People-oriented roles
● Co-ordinator (CO)

The traditional team-leader role is that of co-ordinator. They guide the team to what they perceive are the objectives. They are excellent listeners and are naturally able to recognise the value that each team member brings to the table. As they tend to be calm and good-natured, the co-ordinator can delegate tasks effectively.

Where they are not as strong is in the their tendency to delegate away too much personal responsibility. Others see the continual capacity to involve others and to distribute the workload as simply being manipulative.

● Team worker (TW)

Team workers are those who support others and who make sure the team is working together as well as possible. They will be seen to be flexible and adaptive, capable of negotiation between others and achieving agreement. To the team worker, the people are more important than the prize, and it is their popularity and ability to get along with others than creates an effective social lubricant. Sometimes their desire to support all other team members may lead to a sense that they are indecisive and uncommitted within discussions.

● Resource investigator (RI)

Resource investigators have a curiosity about them and a capacity to innovate. Using contacts and negotiation skills they will make use of all available options and work with external stakeholders to help the team accomplish its objective. Others are often receptive to them and their ideas, often because of their confident and outgoing nature. On the downside, resource investigators are often overly optimistic and may lose enthusiasm quickly if success is not forthcoming.

Thought-oriented roles

● Plant (PL)

The Plant is the person who comes up with new ideas and approaches all the time; they are the creative and imaginative member of the group. Plants may be introverted and can prefer to work apart from the team. Their originality can produce ideas that are impractical at times, as among other things they are not always good communicators and can tend to ignore given parameters and constraints. They thrive on praise, but find criticism hard to deal with.

● Monitor-evaluator (ME)

The Monitor-evaluator is effective at analysing and evaluating the situation – the challenge, the ideas, the actions, the outcomes. They are objective, weighing the pros and cons carefully before coming to a decision. Monitor-evaluators may be seen as remote or uninvolved: this may be due to their very strategic approach and a tendency to react to events rather than instigating them.

● Specialist (SP)

Belbin's work focused on groups with a particular purpose. The Specialist's role is to utilise their specialised knowledge to get the job done. A specialist will know, and be confident about, the match between what is required and what they possess: they are the expert. At times, the focus on the specialised aspects of the task may limit their overall contribution as they are not often disposed towards the 'bigger picture'.

Avoid the mistake of assuming Belbin is suggesting every team must have nine people, each fulfilling a given role. His work makes the argument that teams work better when: (a) there are enough people to fulfil most of the roles; (b) that there is breadth of role within the team; and (c) that individuals have insight into which role they fulfil best.

If you are interested in the sort of Belbin person you might be you will find a variety of Belbin 'rating' or 'scoring' questionnaires readily available on the internet. Most of these are 'modified', because the original materials are only commercially available from the Belbin organisation's website (www.belbin.com). They are usually straightforward and quite fun to do, but you should not over-interpret the outcome or suddenly believe that you need to reinvent yourself because you are advised that you have characteristics of a Belbin type that you did not expect to be.

Tuckman's lifecycle model

A different approach to the understanding of how groups work was presented by Tuckman's lifecycle model. Here, the emphasis is not on group members, but on the stages the group goes through in order to achieve its aim.

A group passes through four lifecycle stages: forming; storming; norming; and performing.

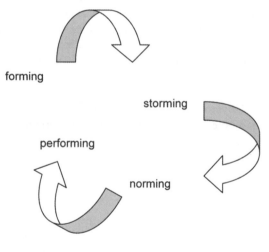

forming

storming

performing

norming

Figure 9.1: Tuckman's (1965) lifecycle of group experience

Forming occurs when a group or team comes together or is formed for the first time. Now there will, of course, be variation in the reasons for the group coming into being, variations in its status, permanence, focus. It may be a group of teachers in the same department, it may be a social group of some sort. There will be a focus on agreeing the purpose of the group and its rules of engagement. The extent to which these are publically articulated will reflect the formal/informal genesis of the group.

The second stage of storming can be seen to be marked by tensions within the group. This can be because of the discerned formation of sub-groups and cliques and a feeling of exclusion (although of course this may be about perception rather than actuality), while coming to terms with the range of interpersonal communication styles within the group members. At the same time, some of the group will be demanding a clearer focus on the group objectives and the strategies for achieving them

Norming, about which much has been already mentioned, is that point at which there is a much stronger sense of cohesion within the group. Informal sanctions may have been applied to establish the consensus, but however it has been done an effective team will by now be sharing a much stronger sense of purpose, even if it remains implicit. Divergent views, expressions of disagreement and even criticism are more manageable because of the more cohesive purpose that has been achieved at this point.

With the emergence of an effective, well-functioning team we have entered the stage of performing. Complex tasks and internal disagreements are dealt with in mature and balanced ways. The group now needs to continue to improve relationships and performance.

You will note that Tuckman's work does not offer timescales for these stages: it is a process, not prescription. An additional stage, added in 1970, was Adjourning. This is particularly important for temporary teams where the group is able to disband when its work is finished and be willing to work together in the future.

There are many more approaches to groups and teams: we have chosen Belbin and Tuckman because their validity does seem to be acknowledged by their longevity. The point we are looking to stress is that you are an individual, but you work in a collaborative organisation. Your own predispositions, values and philosophies may dovetail into the team, department or college of which you are a part, or they may clash noisily with one or more other members. Wherever you find yourself on this continuum your engagement with quality will require an engagement with others.

Teamwork benefits everyone

You will recall from earlier chapters how the quality assurance and quality improvement processes may require scrutiny of success rates, and that these may be considered at the level of individual teacher, course, department or college. Where performance has been well below the expected level, or where there has been little or no improvement over time you can expect some sort of management action plan to be imposed. Again, this might be at the level of the individual teacher or at the level of course team. Given the fraught nature of feelings when people are being professionally criticised you will see the imperative for those involved to respond effectively as a team.

Here again is the call to arms to be proactive and informed in your own approach to quality assurance. While no one likes the show-boating know-all you would be well advised to be fully aware of your learners' success rates, the department success rates and the national success rates, because when the meeting is called to justify or challenge the evaluation that has been applied, or to develop an action plan in response, your manager and your colleagues are going to find more comfort and more confidence in someone who seems to know what is involved and is willing to do something about it. If, in an unfortunate turn of events, your team hasn't achieved any norming and performing but are fragmented and hostile you may as well have your ammunition ready.

But let's not dwell on ineffective teamwork, let's see how you can make a real difference by working well with others.

REFLECTIVE TASK

REFLECTIVE TASK

How is the teaching you deliver in the classroom funded? Who pays and how does your organisation maximise the income to which it might be entitled?

For many staff, until quite recently, the answer would have been the LSC. But now? Local authority? The SFA? The YPLA?

Many teachers may shrug their shoulders and say, 'not my responsibility, that's why we have senior managers'. And to some extent they are right: ever since incorporation, as I mentioned in the tale of the register (see Chapter 1, page 7), the funding models and funding regulations for the sector have been both arcane and ephemeral, and the more financially sound colleges did appoint senior managers who could count and add up. The most recent guidance on funding published by the LSC for 2009/10 ran to 119 pages, and that was only updated guidance, not the original. So there is, without argument, a necessary area of expertise, but that is not a reason to allow prospective and actual teachers to be casual with regard to those aspects of the process on which they can have an influence. For while there has been significant change in terms of the allocation of funds, weightings and extra allowances, there are some fundamental responsibilities that will have a significant impact if the teaching staff overlook them.

CASE STUDY
Working with colleagues for the benefit of all
One aspect of the sector that may pass many teaching staff by is the relationship between success and funding.

I think it is fair to say that for many teachers there is an assumption that once a learner is on a course then all the financial resources that are required are in place and there are no implications for the teacher in terms of securing funding. Nothing could be further from the truth. While manipulated and adjusted from time to time, there is a fundamental link between successful outcomes for learners and what colleges will receive from their various funding agencies.

Take the case of a colleague at my former college.

Between 2003 and 2006 she was given the job of securing outcomes for courses that depended on successful completion of the then Key Skills qualifications, Communication, Application of Number and IT. This was done by a combination of teaching, verifying and administrating. As a successful teacher of Key Skills this colleague was very well acquainted with the course requirement. Moving into an Internal verifier/ Internal moderator role she did not just point out where her colleagues were not facilitating production of the correct evidence at the right level from their learners, she was able to suggest and show how it could be done. She also worked with, and supported, department managers as they sought to create more effective assessment policy and processes.

Bringing to bear her expertise across the Key Skills curriculum she became the lead contact with the External Verifier. Because, over time, the quality of the assessment

---

across the sections and departments clearly improved, the college was awarded Direct Claim Status for its Key Skill awards, meaning that whenever a learner succeeded and had their work signed off internally a claim could be made for the outcome.

Sometimes, the matter was more about simple management of people's capacity to complete the correct forms in due time. It seemed to elude some teachers that, as far as award bodies are concerned, if a learner is not registered with them they don't exist – even if they are sitting in front of you in a classroom. And if they are not registered you will be unable to identify an outcome, unable to claim funding for it and risk a poor success rate score.

The following table shows what was achieved in terms of the increase in the number of successful outcomes.

Key Skill	03/04 outcomes	05/06 outcomes
Communication	129	601
Application of Number	152	382
ITC	94	581
Total increase in successful outcomes (including some difference in actual number of entries)		1189

Table 9.2: Numbers of portfolios successfully claimed

So, what was achieved by one person's ability to work effectively with others?

Well clearly, there would be an impact on the self-esteem of those achieving a qualification that previously – for whatever reason – might not have been achieved. The self-esteem and confidence of teachers might improve as they see the impact of their work on the outcomes for their learners.

College success rates would improve, generating data that could be fed into the overall Self-evaluation Report and would be considered most favourably by Ofsted. Oh, and the small matter of more funding to be claimed, in the region of an extra £50,000 – this being the difference between funding for learners being on the course and the element of funding retained by the LSC and paid on successful completion.

That's the salary for two new teachers.

REFLECTIVE TASK

Just think about it: getting your assessment and administration right contributes directly to job security. Bit of a 'no-brainer', really.

A SUMMARY OF **KEY POINTS**

In this chapter we have:

> examined the nature of collaboration within a teaching role in the sector;

> considered the impact of social influence as it shapes organisations and their culture;

> provided an introduction to the work of Belbin on team roles and the work of Tuckman on team development;

> identified those colleagues who will be significant partners in your work;

> highlighted just how fundamental to the financial health of a college effective teamwork will be.

REFERENCES REFERENCES REFERENCES REFERENCES REFERENCES REFERENCES

Belbin, M (1981) *Management Teams*. London: Heinemann.

Homans, G (1975) *The Human Group.* London: Routledge & Kegan Paul.

Knights, D and Willmott, H (eds.) (2007) *Introducing Organisational Behaviour and Management.* London: Thomson Learning.

Schein, E H (2004) *Organisational Culture and Leadership.* San Francisco, CA: Jossey-Bass.

Tuckman, B (1965) Developmental Sequence in Small Groups. *Psychological Bulletin*, 63: 384–99.

10
Putting it all together

This chapter is designed to:

- provide you with a review of the issues raised so far;
- facilitate reflection on your own experience of quality assurance and quality improvement;
- identify the strategies to underwrite your involvement in quality assurance and quality improvement;
- develop an informed critical approach to create the most appropriate personal response.

It addresses the following Professional Standards for QTLS:

AS 4 Reflection and evaluation of their own practice and their continuing professional development as teachers.

AS 7 Improving the quality of their practice.

AK 4.3 Ways to reflect, evaluate and use research to develop own practice, and to share good practice with others.

AK 7.2 Own role in the quality cycle.

AK 7.3 Ways to implement improvements based on feedback received.

BK 2.6 Ways to evaluate own practice in terms of efficiency and effectiveness.

FS 4 A multi-agency approach to supporting development and progression opportunities for learners.

Introduction

Quality is not done to you; quality is owned.
(Steve Roberts, former Director of Quality, Barnsley College, South Yorkshire)

REFLECTIVE TASK

Consider the themes we have covered across the chapters in this text.

- In Chapter 1, understanding the concept, origins and application of quality assurance, evaluation and quality improvement in the sector.

- In Chapter 2, establishing key strategies to ensure delivery of excellent teaching.

- In Chapters 3 and 4, considering how to prepare for and benefit from internal and external inspection.

- In Chapter 5, scrutiny of the purpose and practice of assessment and the quality assurance of this.

- In Chapter 6, considering authentic ways to evaluate the learners' experience, capture their voice and to respond to their feedback.

- In Chapters 7 and 8, looking at the creation of ethos and values and how these inform individual professionalism and accountability.

- In Chapter 9, individual and collective responsibility within successful teamwork.

To what extent do you think these developments can be shown to have a constructive and beneficial impact on the aspiration to improve the quality of the teaching and learning within the sector?

While you might not be convinced by every policy and process that has been developed, there is at least a broad framework of approaches that carry some useful tools/processes. These, in turn, can be seen to generate some data that, in the right hands, can inform and improve practice within and beyond the classroom, workshop and work place.

What we have been seeking to provide in this text is a description of the blend of quality strategy and quality practice as it has evolved and been established. We recognise there are some fundamental challenges in applying models of quality assurance and quality improvement, originating in manufacturing, to a human process such as teaching and learning. Fundamentally, there is a merging of two environments: one partially animate, that of manufacturing, where the raw materials merely have things done to them and where the variability is more likely to be found in the operatives; and one wholly animate, that of education, where both essential components, teachers and learners, are unpredictable and ever changeable.

Those issues notwithstanding, we have to recognise the development of those models of quality assurance and quality improvement that have been applied to the challenging arena of post-compulsory education and training in the early twenty-first century. What is fundamental is to generate a sense of ownership of the practice and process and to provide the necessary signposting to how you can most effectively achieve this personal ownership. Let's revisit our themes, gathering them together into three broad groups.

1. The concept and utilisation of quality in post-compulsory education and training

There is no doubt that anyone who has ever sat in a classroom, at whatever age, can tell you clearly and passionately about who was a 'good' teacher and what was a 'bad' lesson, but that's not the same as having the agreed measures that would begin to fit into the sort of quality management framework, drawn from the approaches prevalent in industry, that has become the established template within the sector. There are, of course, many popular conceptions of measuring whether or not a school or college could be classed as 'good': for example, how many exams passed; how many jobs gained by leavers; how many expulsions; how many underage pregnancies; how many times did the police visit in a term; how often did children offer their seat to the elderly on the bus or train; how often did they wear their uniform smartly; how many trophies won. We are a pluralist society and there are many concepts of good in whatever context you wish to consider. But in addition, whatever measure you choose, there are always many qualifying factors, always caveats: well it depends on the children; it depends on the parents; it depends on where you live; it depends on the government; it depends on the experts. So where does this leave us all on our search for quality?

We have to recognise a fundamental tension within quality assurance and quality improvement and that is the issue of 'ownership': it pervades all our chapters and is redolent in the forums and blogs you will come across in your studies or CPD. It can be captured in the question: 'Are we doing this to make a real difference or just manage our reputation?'

REFLECTIVE TASK
REFLECTIVE TASK

Which motor vehicle manufacturer suffered the biggest loss in reputation between 2009 and 2010?

If your answer wasn't Toyota, where have you been for the last two years?

Toyota, the company with *the* leading reputation for quality control and which, in professional and popular opinion, had the most reliable range of cars of any high volume manufacturer, had a most spectacular fall from grace with the recall of millions of vehicles – at a cost of more than $2 billion (*Guardian*, 17 February 2010) – that appeared to have problems with sticking accelerators and in some cases failing brakes.

Leading commentators have reflected on the irony of an organisation seen as a leading light in quality control compounding its difficulties by poorly thought out and poorly executed responses to the dilemma. Part of the problem was tension between quality assurance of the product and the quality assurance of the reputation (Diermeier, 2010).

Quality as marketing

Travelling down the major ring road in Liverpool you would pass three schools in the space of one and half miles. Each proudly declaims its quality in terms of Ofsted judgements on banners several metres high and wide.

Have you received a letter from a school or college recently? Did you notice citation of Ofsted's most recent judgement?

Have a look at the adverts on the sides of buses: particularly over the summer as young people consider their future choices. There will be significant presence of college adverts seeking to persuade and recruit: many will be making claims based on a recent Ofsted report or on their achievement of results or their place in the 'league' table.

The prevalence of such material is not restricted to education: there is no doubt a fruitful and interesting sociology or media thesis already written that analyses the changes in the use of 'quality' as a marketing tool. And this is one of the core challenges in the effective development of quality assurance and quality improvement: most teachers will happily engage with the process if they believe it will inform the decision-making and resourcing necessary to improve teaching and learning. However, when they see what they consider to be a hijacking of the process in order to provide some 'sound-bite', their commitment and enthusiasm can wither.

Another complaint, common among every workforce since the advent of quality assurance within 'service' industries, has been the amount of paperwork and form-filling that appear to be a requirement, rather than 'doing the job'.

> ### CASE STUDY
> An extract from Dave Willets' (then Shadow Minster for Education) speech to Association of Colleges, 19 November 2009.
>
> *Every college Principal I meet tells me they have literally dozens of staff whose job is to collect data for a multiplicity of regulators and funding bodies which is not needed for the good management of the college. At one leading college I visited recently, they said they have to fill in more than 200 data fields for every enrolment (average of three enrolments per learner), have a lever-arch binder full of paper for each Train to Gain learner and have 45 staff who work exclusively on collecting and entering data. Under our model, much of this can be swept away. Tough times lie ahead. This is where the savings have to be made. I don't want to read of cuts to courses when there are still lots of administrators collecting data that is not essential to your core mission.*

Now that clearly is a politician's enticement, but the appeal to 'less paperwork' is an attractive and resonant one. However, whatever the nuances of policy and process, whatever the colour or blend of the political leaders, the core items of quality assurance are well embedded in the sector now and you will be required to engage with them, so below is a checklist of key materials and interactions.

PRACTICAL TASK PRACTICAL TASK PRACTICAL TASK PRACTICAL TASK PRACTICAL TASK

Preparing for your engagement with quality

Have you seen any of the following? Do you have your own copies of them?

- Scheme of Work and Lesson Plan templates.
- Lesson/subject evaluation pro-formas.
- Module/course evaluation pro-formas.
- Course/college satisfaction questionnaires.
- Your award body's Chief Examiner or Lead Verifier report for your subject.
- 'League' tables showing your subject benchmarks and the college's overall performance.
- A course/team/department/college Self-assessment report.
- Your organisation's last Ofsted report.
- Your organisation's subsequent action plan.

Have you had a conversation about quality assurance and quality improvement with any of the following?

- Your immediate colleagues.
- Your team leader.
- Your line manager.
- Your subject coach or mentor.
- Your organisation's management team.

As we have been stressing all along, while these processes and the attendant paperwork are not without some flaws, they are in place and you will be needing to engage with them. The subsequent conversations must be owned by you.

2. The quality of teaching, learning and assessment

From Chapters 2 to 5 we have explored questions about how to recognise and develop excellent teaching, how you will experience both internal and external inspections and the processes, again both internal and external, that are in place to secure the fairest and most equitable assessment strategies.

Actions to take to quality assure your own teaching

Know and understand the figures

Don't hide from the data. We started with W. Edwards Deming and we will revisit him now. Data is not maths – data is understanding what some figures tell you. Are you doing what can be fairly called a 'good' job given the curriculum, the learners, the resources, national trends and standards? Can your knowledge of the data inform the discussion of your performance as a teacher that will be considered by both internal and external inspections?

A key agency will be the Data Service, funded by the Department for Business, Innovation and Skills with a remit to act as a single point of information for the sector. Its role is described as *managing the collection, transformation and dissemination of all further education data, and to being responsive to the changing data needs of the sector* (Data Service, 2010).

Here regular reports will be published, so if you want to know how your curriculum area or your subject is performing nationally in terms of success rates this is the place to go. You can also use the archives of the LSC website for older records.

We are not denying that there needs to be scrutiny and argument about the validity, reliability and interpretation of those measures that have become part of the quality landscape. However, if you choose not to develop a basic cognisance of the figures you do run the risk of being perhaps unfairly criticised by someone with little or no discernment themselves. And we see little or no defence against having some informed knowledge of the patterns and trends in your learners' achievements.

Enhance your subject knowledge

Be proactive in sourcing teaching and learning materials. Join your professional association: nearly every subject has one and membership is often free or reduced for students. Here you will find a wide range of material designed and developed by colleagues working in your subject-specific field. There may be variation in the quality, some materials may need updating and contextualising, but at least here is a starting point and contact with colleagues whose professionalism commits them to share best practice rather than hide it away. Many associations will have conferences and workshops at relatively little cost. Use some leverage of quality assurance, quality improvement and CPD to seek financial support from your employer in maintaining currency in your expertise. Here are some of the major subject areas represented.

Association of Hairdressers and Therapists	www.aht-uk.org
Association for Physical Education	www.afpe.org.uk
Association of Teachers of Mathematics	www.atm.org.uk
Institute of Engineering and Technology	www.theiet.org/
National Association for the Teaching of English	www.nate.org.uk
National Association of Music Educators	www.name.org.uk
National Association of Plumbing Teachers	www.napt-plumbing-teachers.org.uk
National Drama	www.nationaldrama.co.uk
The Association of Teachers of Psychology	www.theatp.org
The Association for Science Education	www.ase.org.uk
The Association of Law Teachers	www.lawteacher.ac.uk
The Association of Social Science Teachers	www.atss.org.uk
The Economics, Business and Enterprise Association	www.ebea.org.uk
The Historical Association	www.history.org.uk
The ICT Association (NAACE)	www.naace.org.uk
The National Society for Education in Art and Design	www.nsead.org
The Professional Association for Catering Education	www.keepinpace.org

Table 10.1: Subject-specific organisations

An effective search strategy to use is a combination of the terms 'Association', 'Teachers' and a given subject specialism. There may be some subject where a UK-based association seems to be missing, for example Agricultural Education, but it doesn't mean the websites and resources of international bodies are completely without benefit, e.g. the National Association of Agricultural Educators based in Australia will at least provide ideas.

If there isn't an association or professional body then why not look for a blog or forum as a starting point.

Improve your knowledge of assessment strategies and skills in making assessment decisions

After two or three years working in the sector, whether full-time or part-time, apply to become an Assistant Examiner or Assistant Moderator for your subject. Look on the relevant award body website for appointment opportunities and how to apply. While it does involve more work you will become significantly more competent as a teacher, certainly in terms of assessment of learning. You gain confidence in interpreting the syllabus or specification and in conveying to your learners the level and nature of the questions that are set and so improving their overall preparation for assessment.

If you are teaching vocational subjects look to achieve your Assessor Award(s) and then to move on to the Verifier Award.

To further enhance your status and your involvement in assessment, join the Chartered Institute of Educational Assessors, www.ciea.org.uk.

Keep up to date with the sector as a whole

Read the educational press regularly (not just the job pages). *The Times Educational Supplement* has an FE sector pull-out each week and the *Guardian* education supplement also covers FE frequently. Use the many websites and blogs that cover the topic of post-compulsory education and training. The BBC website has a link to articles and commentary on education that don't necessarily make the news headlines.

You also have the opportunity to join a trades union, the major one being the University and College Union (UCU), www.ucu.org.uk, and a smaller one being the Association of Teachers and Lecturers (ATL), www.atl.org.uk. As well as campaigning for conditions of service and providing a voice in the national debate over education, a trades union is an excellent reference point for information regarding trends and innovations in the section, a barometer of what the next big idea might be.

It doesn't have to be this way

We have set before you the likely parameters of quality assurance within which you will probably work. They are not perfect and they need robust and resolute critical appraisal to be continually applied. If you can find the time and confidence to adopt this approach you will not only be equipped to comply with requirements that may be imposed, but you will also develop sufficient critical faculties to take the best from quality assurance and quality improvement strategies and use them to evaluate your own practice and to improve it where required. Own it, don't let quality be done to you.

3.The collaborative nature of quality – the student voice, personal professionalism and organisational effectiveness

Too many organisations seem to be intent on manipulating the student voice rather than listening to it. In so doing they sadly highlight the fact that teachers, and more particularly their managers, lack discernment about certain aspects of modern-day life.

For example, the post-compulsory sector is part of the wider coalition of Lifelong Learning and Skills. Many of its learners are mature, informed and insightful. If you ask them to engage in audits, evaluations and consultations then they will speak their mind. If, having spoken their mind, their feedback is diluted or reinterpreted to reduce the possibility of more tendentious comments then, when presented with the published versions of such quality tools, one finds an even more critical response fired by the indignation that their requested opinions have been apparently tampered with. This is not to condone poor organisation and poor administration with regard to conducting such evaluative events or processes in such a way as to allow a negative minority to dominate the feedback. It is salutary to note that if you ask your learners to identify positive aspects of your work or your department's work, then they will do so, and there is every reason for designing the tools and conducting the meetings in a way that fairly captures this. However, if the majority of the feedback message is not positive, then organisations need to ask themselves why this might be, rather than pour energy into creating a more attractive interpretation of the information provided.

The enthusiasm for managing bad news is also susceptible to the informed and imaginative use that learners make of the media if they wish to express their dissatisfaction, as we can see in the next case study.

CASE STUDY
Facebook protests over A level exams

Facebook protest groups against A level exams taken this week have spread with complaints about a biology paper from another exam board.

The AQA biology exam taken on Monday prompted an instant online protest with claims that the questions were unfair. Another protest on the social networking website is now raising concerns about an OCR A level biology also taken on Monday.

> *The Ofqual qualifications watchdog has called for a report on the concerns.*
>
> (Coughlan, 2010)

> *584 students have now joined a Facebook campaign to protest against the nature of their A level English Literature examination.*
>
> (Baker, 2010)

Hard to keep the lid on bad news these days. So, rather than put the energy into managing the adverse messages, it might be a novel approach to put the effort into delivering the product better in the first place.

That is not to say that as a profession teachers in the sector could not become a little more comfortable with being held to account for their responsibilities.

CASE STUDY
Kodak and the candid feedback

In the late 1980s, because of my tentative involvement with teacher training, I was asked by my college to write a two-day course for staff at the local Kodak factory. They were moving to a multi-tasking model of maintenance where specialist divisions – gas, electrical, plumbing – would train each other in some core skills so that work would not be held up unnecessarily if a full complement of engineers were not present. I was admittedly somewhat naive and it had not occurred to me just how much resistance there would be to this breaking down of well-established lines of professional demarcation. Nevertheless, with a colleague I wrote and delivered a two-day course that involved a lot about teaching aliens to make tea and playing with Lego as I recall.

The key learning point for me was that, after we had finished and had packed up, the Personnel Manager called me into his office before I left. He thanked me for the course, said his staff had enjoyed it and felt it had achieved much of what they had wanted. He then said, very directly, 'I think you should know that the feedback from staff was that you were the much stronger character, the better teacher and more effective in helping them achieve.' Both surprised and flattered by this, and not a little embarrassed for my friend and colleague, I made my thanks and left.

I had been teaching for about eight years at this point and had never experienced anything as specific and direct as this in terms of my teaching performance. Sure, students said nice things to you if and when they passed their exams, and Christmas or the end of year might bring some 'thank you' gifts. But somehow, this level of candid comment was not the 'done thing'.

It is worth noting that neither my colleague nor I had asked the participants what they thought of the course – not something that was done at the time. It certainly didn't help that the Personnel Manager had sounded as if he wanted me to do something to

---

improve my colleague's performance. There wasn't really a climate in our college of robust, professional discussion. I had joined a staffroom where the prevailing attitude was one of staff superiority over students and of inviolate reputation: had they all known about the BBS in the case study described in Chapter 6 perhaps they would have been less over-confident.

On reflection I realised that here was a different culture, one dependent on commercial success and effective management for its economic viability and long-term future: why shouldn't they have a point of view about the quality of what they had paid for and received? And, as an organisation needing to receive and respond to its own customers' feedback, there was no doubt that the Personnel Manager expected this to be an established and welcome practice within education.

(I never told my friend about this, so Malcolm, if you're reading this now, buck your ideas up.)

PRACTICAL TASK PRACTICAL TASK PRACTICAL TASK PRACTICAL TASK PRACTICAL TASK

Build in the opportunity to collect current feedback from your learners. Plan it now, not at the end of term or after exams. You can make this specific – ask what they think about the quality of hand-outs, PowerPoint slides, textbooks chosen, and so on. Or you can make it broad – ask what they think about the teaching and learning strategies in general, your communication style, your approachability; whatever you feel comfortable with.

Don't make it onerous and do it in an atmosphere of a dialogue. Trust them: even if it is not going well most learners will look to give feedback that helps rather than just criticise.

REFLECTIVE TASK
REFLECTIVE TASK

- What was the outcome? How does it chime with other measures of the student voice that your organisation currently uses?
- Could you make it a regular small-scale activity that could be used every week?
- How do you think it might change the learning dialogue between you and your learners?

It could be argued that this is an inherently more professional approach to teaching than the mandatory membership of a government-sponsored body. There needs to be thoughtful evaluation of the IfL as the professional body for the sector as its existence seems to imply that anyone teaching in the sector before 2007 could not have been a proper 'professional' because they did not have a set of standards by which to be judged, or an organisation to join. Established as part of the 2004 White Paper (DfES, 2004), one of the principal focuses of the IfL has been to act as the agency scrutinising its members' requirement to participate in a minimum of 30 hours CPD each year.

Opinion within the sector seems rather divided on this process: some resent the obligatory nature of something they have considered intrinsically part of their role, while others welcome the structuring and sharing of the CPD experience. If you have completed your initial teacher training since 2007 you will have no choice, you will need to join the IfL in order to achieve your ATLS or QTLS status through the process of Professional Formation.

Teachers who qualified before 2007 are encouraged to consider membership of the IfL and applying for QTLS:

> The IfL is encouraging all those teaching in the Learning and Skills sector to achieve this as a demonstration of professionalism. The licence will be conferred subject to successful completion of professional formation.
>
> (IfL, 2010)

However, like many other 'professional bodies', one cannot help but detect a punitive, legalistic approach to the whole concept of professionalism: it is almost as if you need to have it so we can take it away. Thus, it is disappointing to see that while some prominence is given on the IfL website to the 'Code of Professional Practice', a one-page document, a visitor to the site is quickly directed to how to complain using the 'Code of Practice Raising Concerns about IfL Members', a 15-page document.

As far back as 1993, Holmes was pointing to the limitations of such models as TQM and of management-driven approaches to quality which 'professionalise'. He argued for the need for a collegial model that accepts the central importance of interactive professionalism in assuring real quality of teaching and learning. The IfL appears to be the beginning of this collegial model, but if they are drawn too far down the road of policing then they become another management-driven process. There is an argument that if you don't need to have the concept of being a professional explained to you then you are one, while if you need it explaining you will probably never become one.

So do not be surprised if you come across ambivalence towards the IfL in the work place: most staff did train and qualify before 2007 and it may be some time before IfL members become a majority. Which brings us back to the collaborative nature of work in the sector: sometimes it flourishes, sometimes it doesn't. As with so many aspects of quality under discussion you have to take ownership of your role and your subsequent responsibilities. As Buchholz and Roth (1987) point out: *Wearing the same shirts doesn't make you a team.*

A final critical point – performativity

Balls defines performativity as, *a technology, a culture and a mode of regulation that employs judgements, comparisons and displays as a means of incentive, control, attrition and change* (2003, page 216).

Incentive, control, attrition, change: a utilitarian reduction to measurable commodities, education simply reduced to recruitment rates, retention rates, success rates and league tables, bouquets and brickbats to drive forward change. And for 'change' read improvement, because someone somewhere will have promised it. Coffield (2008) calls it the *acquisition metaphor of learning*, only ever seeing the whole experience of education, at whatever life stage, as nothing more than acquiring a certificate via a process of assessment. And despite our implied criticism throughout this book that quality has emerged from business, in both its management and manufacturing guises, and is somehow tainted by this, it is interesting to note that those immersed in the world of business seem to agree with the Balls and Coffield critique. Alan Chapman, author of the BusinessBalls website, provides this telling commentary:

Testing ... is used to assess and pronounce people's fundamental worth – which quite obviously directly affects self-esteem, confidence, ambition, dreams, life purpose, etc. (nothing too serious then ...).

Perhaps most significantly, if you fail to develop people as individuals, and only aim to transfer knowledge and skills to meet the organisational priorities of the day, then you will seriously hamper your chances of fostering a happy productive society within your workforce, assuming you want to, which I guess is another subject altogether.

(Chapman, 2010)

REFLECTIVE TASK

What is post-compulsory education and training really about?

Conclusion

So how do we identify and measure best practice in quality assurance and quality improvement in post-compulsory education and training? And if we can achieve this, how can we make best use of the information to improve practice? And who should own the process and where does responsibility lie?

The purpose of this book has been to try to answer some of those questions and, in so doing, enliven and enlighten those prospective new teachers in the post-compulsory sector.

Having been active in initial teacher training for the sector for 20 years now and in post-compulsory education (both further and higher) for nearly 30 years, I believe strongly that, while nothing is more important that a well-planned, well-resourced lesson delivered by an enthusiastic teacher who knows their stuff, we will be doing a disservice to our teacher training students if we do not prepare them for the practice and process of quality assurance and quality improvement in whatever form it may take. There is no doubt that, despite national polices and practice, local interpretation and application is as varied as the number of colleges themselves. One consequence is that many teachers new to the sector are at first surprised and then alarmed at the amount of non-teaching related administration with which they have to engage.

It has been the intention of the authors to provide a clear framework to the most obvious quality assurance policy and practice and to equip new teachers with the willingness to undertake, and indeed take ownership of, those elements that genuinely make a difference to the student experience. Alongside this we have shone a light on those spurious, performative, target-driven excesses so beloved of the 'league table' managers and attempted to equip our readers with the confidence to raise professional criticisms of the same while not neglecting their contractual responsibilities. Good luck.

A SUMMARY OF **KEY POINTS**

In this chapter we have:

> reviewed the issues raised so far;

> asked you to reflect on your own experience of quality assurance and quality improvement to date;

> suggested that there are strategies you can pursue that will guarantee the quality of your own work, irrespective of organisational policy and procedures;

> encouraged you to develop an informed critical approach that combines your professional commitment to quality with a healthy scepticism of the manipulation of quality 'data'.

REFERENCES REFERENCES REFERENCES REFERENCES REFERENCES REFERENCES

Baker, M (2010) www.mikebakereducation.co.uk/blog/239/facebook-protest-over-aqa-english-exam/

Ball, S J (2003) The Teacher's Soul and the Terrors of Performativity. *Journal of Educational Policy,* 18 (2): 215–28.

Buchholz, S and Roth, T (1987) *Creating the High Performance Team*. New York: Wiley.

Chapman, A (2010) *Lessons From (and Perhaps Also For) Children's Education.* www.businessballs. com/trainingprogramevaluation.htm (accessed July 2010).

Coffield, F (2008) *Just Suppose Teaching and Learning Became the First Priority.* London: Learning and Skills Network.

Coughlan, S (2010) Facebook Campaign against A-level Exam Paper. http://news.bbc.co.uk/1/hi/education/8480563.stm

Data Service (2010) www.thedataservice.co.uk/

DfES (2004) *Equipping Our Teachers for the Future: Reforming Initial Teacher Training for the Lifelong Learning Sector*. London: HMSO.

Diermeier, (2010) The Toyota Recall: Understanding the Real Problem. www.businessweek.com/managing/content/feb2010/ca2010029_503075.htm (accessed August 2010).

Holmes, G (1993) Quality Assurance in Further and Higher Education: A Sacrificial Lamb on the Altar of Managerialism. *Quality Assurance in Education,* 1: 4–8.

Ifl (2010) www.ifl.ac.uk/about-ifl/faq (accessed August 2010).

Index

Added to the page reference 'f' denotes a figure and 't' denotes a table.

A level curriculum, and the politicisation of assessment 50
A Toolkit for Creative Teaching in Post Compulsory Education 20
A1 – Vocational Assessor Award 99
50 Templates for Teaching and Learning 20
accelerated learning 16
accountability, professionalism 90–1
achievement, as a measure of outcomes 58
acquisition metaphor of learning 124
action plans/reviews 40
active learning 16
Advanced Learning Coach (ALC) status 26
Advanced Practitioners (APs), case study 25–6
aims and objectives for lessons 16, 18
appropriate dress for teachers 94
assessment 49–60
  case study 52–3
  components of QA in 53–6
    Centre Risk Assessment (CRA) 55–6
    Direct Claim Status (DCS) 55, 56
    moderation 53–4
    'Value Added' (VA) and 'Distance Travelled' (DT) 59, 72
    verification 54–5
  defining 4
  improving knowledge of strategies of and skills in making decisions on 120
  outcomes 57–9
    success rates *see* success rates
  as a politicised process 50–3
    casualties 50–1
    employers' views 51–2
    teachers' reactions 51
  teacher involvement in the QA and QI of 56–7
    case study 56–7
  uses 49–50
  see also formative assessment; interim assessments; self-assessment; summative assessment
assessment of learning 49–50
assessment for learning 50
associate teachers 97
autonomy 91
awarding bodies 36

becoming a community 83–4
  see also inclusive practice
behaviour of teachers, appropriate 94–5
Belbin's team roles model 108–10
  action oriented roles 108
  people oriented roles 108–9
  'rating' or 'scoring' questionnaires 110
  thought oriented roles 109
beliefs, shared 78–9
Bipolar scale approaches 67
BTEC awards, use of Centre Risk Assessment (CRA) 55–6

care
  as a principle of the IfL code of professional practice 93
  see also duty-of-care obligations
caring, community of 77–8
case studies
  Advanced Practitioners (APs) 25–6
  assessment 52–3
  college/organisation culture 105
    sub-cultures within 80
  effective teamwork and financial health 112–13
  inclusive practice 84–5
  internal inspection 40–1
  IQER (Integrated Quality and Enhancement Review) 37
  learner voice 65, 122
  observation process 24, 42–3

Ofsted inspections 34
personal professionalism and
    organisational effectiveness 122–3
professionalism 101–2
safeguarding young people and
    vulnerable adults 101
self-regulation 47–8
teacher involvement in the QA and QI
    of assessment 56–7
use of registers 7–8
CBI (Confederation of British Industry),
    views on school leavers 51–2
celebration of success 82
Centre Risk Assessment (CRA) 55–6
ceremonies and college/organisation
    culture 79
Certificate in Assessing Candidates Using
    a Range of Methods (A1 – Vocational
    Assessor Award) 99
Certificate in Education/Certificate in
    Higher Education (Cert Ed/Cert HE) 98
Certificate in Teaching in the Lifelong
    Learning Sector (CTLLS) 97
checking learning 17, 23–4
CIF (Common Inspection Framework)
    (2009) 10, 31
classroom, quality in 14–26
co-ordinators in teams 108–9
codes of practice 91
    see also IfL code of professional
        practice
collaborative nature of quality 121–4
collective versus individual responsibility
    105
college/organisation culture 75–8
    defining indicators 78–9
        heroes and heroines 79
        networks of players 79
        rituals, ceremonies and stories 79
        shared values and beliefs 78–9
    effect of attitudes and beliefs 76, 105–7
        case study 105
    effect of relationships 77–8
    effect of a shared vision 77
    impact 76
    influence of cultural norms 77
    sub-cultures within 79
        case study 80
Common Inspection Framework (CIF)
    (2009) 10, 31

communication process 81–2
    channel 81
    context 82
    feedback 82
    message 81
    receiver 81
    sender 81
communication skills
    importance 80
    removing barriers 81–2
community
    becoming 82–4
    becoming a, see also inclusive practice
community of caring 77–8
completer-finishers in teams 108
concepts of quality 1–12
    recognising 3–5
    utilisation and 116–19
Conduct Internal Quality Assurance of the
    Assessment Process (V1 – Vocational
    Internal Verifiers Award) 99
Confederation of British Industry (CBI),
    views on school leavers 51–2
Continuing Professional Development
    (CPD) 92, 123
course programme evaluation by students
    68, 70–1
CRA (Centre Risk Assessment) 55–6
creative teachers 19–20
*The Creative Teaching and Learning
    Toolkit* 20
criminal offence disclosure *see* disclosure
Crosby, Philip 6
CTLLS (Certificate in Teaching in the
    Lifelong Learning Sector) 97
cultural norms, effect on college/
    organisation culture 77
culture of colleges *see* college/
    organisation culture
curriculum, and inclusive practice 86–7

data 1
    evaluation 1–2
    knowing and understanding 119
    measurement *see* measurement of
        data
    see also success rates
Data Service 119
deadlines, meeting 95
definition of quality 2–3

Deming, W. Edwards 1, 6
differentiation 21, 84, 94
    defining 83
Diploma in Teaching in the Lifelong
    Learning Sector (DTLLS) 97–8
Direct Claim Status (DCS) 55, 56
disclosure 95
    as a principle of the IfL code of
        professional practice 93
'Distance Travelled' (DT) 59, 72
dress for teachers, appropriate 94
Duran, Joseph 6
duty-of-care obligations 95

ECM (Every Child Matters) agenda 86
Edexcel Centre Risk Assessment (CRA)
    Policy 55–6
Education and Inspection Act (2006) 30
effective teamwork 104–5, 107–11
    and financial health 112–13
        case study 112–13
    models 107–11
EMAs 85
employers' views 51–2, 63
environment
    creating a safer 100
    and inclusive practice 86
ethos
    defining 78
    and inclusive practice 86
    sharing 80–2
        through celebrating success 82
        through communication skills *see*
        communication skills
ETS Europe 50
evaluation
    of data 1–2
    defining 4
    of the learners' experience *see* student
        evaluation
    philosophy 66–7
    of staff 41
Every Child Matters (ECM) agenda 87
excellence, achieving 39
external inspection 9–10, 28–38, 40–1
    by Ofsted *see* Ofsted inspections
    Framework for Excellence (FfE) *see*
        Framework for Excellence (FfE)
    IQER (Integrated Quality and
        Enhancement Review) 36–7

case study 37
external moderation 53–4
external verification 54, 55

feedback
    in the communication process 82
    from learners 17, 40, 48
    giving 43–4
    informal 66
feedback sandwich technique 43–4
Feigenbaum, Armand 6
financial support for learners 86
form-filling, paperwork and *see*
    paperwork and form-filling
formative assessment 17, 23
four level model of evaluation,
    Kirkpatrick's 71
'The Fourteen Steps to Quality
    Improvement' 6
Framework for Excellence (FfE) 11, 35
    Effectiveness dimension 58
    indicators 63
    and the stakeholder voice 62–4
*From Little Acorns: Towards a Strategy
    for Spreading Good Practice Within
    Colleges* 25
'full teaching role', definition 97–8
funding 8
    for learners 86
    link with quality 9, 42, 56, 87, 112–13
        case study 112–13
funding bodies 9

handouts 19
heroes and heroines 78
hierarchical feedback 44
Higher Education Funding Council for
    England (HEFCE) 36

IfL 92
    evaluation of 123–4
IfL code of professional practice 93
    in practice 94–5
    sanctions for breaching 93
implementers in teams 108
inclusion agenda, coping with 83
inclusive practice
    case study 84–5
    defining 83
    supporting 85–8

with resources 87
    support for learners 85–6
    through the curriculum 86–7
    through ethos and environment 87
    through participation 87–8
inclusive teaching 83
Incorporation of post-compulsory
    education 8–9
Individual Target Grades (ITGs) 59
individual versus collective responsibility
    105
informal feedback 66
inspection regimes 9–10
    see also external inspection; internal
        inspection; Ofsted
Institute for Learning *see* IfL
integrity, as a principle of the IfL code of
    professional practice 93
interim assessments 31
internal inspection 39–48
    case study 40–1
    observation *see* observation
    self-assessment 45–6
    self-regulation 46–8
        case study 47–8
    systems 44
internal moderation 53
internal verification 54, 55
IQER (Integrated Quality and
    Enhancement Review) 36–7
    case study 37
ISO 9000 4
ITGs (Individual Target Grades) 59

Kirkpatrick's four level model of
    evaluation 71
'knowledge brokers', case study 25–6

leadership 7
league tables 50, 59
learner voice 61–73, 121–2
    case study 122
    discerning 65
        case study 65
    engagement of providers with 64
    evaluation *see* student evaluation
    power of 63
learners
    feedback from 17, 40, 48
    support for 85–6

valuing 94
learning
    checking 17, 23–4
    observation of *see* observation
    personalised approach 21–2, 59
    planning for *see* planning for learning
    see also accelerated learning;
        acquisition metaphor of learning;
        active learning
'Learning Questionnaires' 67
Learning and Skills Improvement Service
    (LSIS) 11, 26
Learning and Skills Improvement Service
    (LSIS) Excellence Gateway 11–12
lessons
    aims and objectives 16, 18
    being early for 94
    finishing on time 94
    quality *see* quality lessons
    resources 19–20, 94
    structure 15–17
lifecycle of group experience, Tuckman's
    see Tuckman's lifecycle model
Lifelong Learning UK (LLUK) professional
    standards 92
Likert scale approaches 67
listening to learners *see* learner voice
litigation culture 66
LSC Framework for Excellence (FfE) *see*
    Framework for Excellence (FfE)

MAG (Minimum Acceptable Grades) 59
marketing, quality as 117
measurement of data 1, 116
    achievement 58
    retention 57
    success *see* success rates
Minimum Levels of Performance Reports
    (MLPs) 58
moderation 53–4
module evaluation forms 68, 69f
module/subject evaluation by learners 67–
    8
monitor-evaluators in teams 109
MTG (Minimum Target Grades) 59

National tests 51
networks of players and college/
    organisation culture 79
North West Quality Network 7, 10

objectives for lessons, aims and 16, 18
observation 24–5, 41–3
   case studies 24, 42–3
   giving feedback on 43–4
Office of Qualifications and Examinations
   Regulation (Ofqual) 51
Ofsted 30
Ofsted Common Inspection Framework
   (CIF) (2009) 10, 31
Ofsted grading standards, criteria for
   planning lessons 19, 21, 22, 23, 24
Ofsted inspections 30–1, 45
   case study 34
   experiences of 32–4
   frequency 31
   grading criteria 30, 41
   learner and employer involvement 31
   notice given 31
   publication of reports 31
organisational culture *see* college/
   organisation culture
organisational effectiveness, *see* personal
   professionalism and organisational
   effectiveness
outcomes from assessment 57–9
   success rates *see* success rates
outstanding teachers 14, 22
ownership
   concept 61, 66, 116
   of outcomes of student evaluation 71–3

paperwork and form-filling 117–19
   case study 118
   see also record keeping
participation, and inclusive practice 87–8
performativity 124–5
personal professionalism and
   organisational effectiveness 122–4
   case study 122–3
personalisation 21–2, 59
Peters, Tom 7
PGCE (Professional Graduate Certificate in
   Education) 98–9
philosophy of student evaluation 66–7
Plan/Do/Check/Act cycle 6
planning for learning 15–19, 94
   rationale 18
   structure 15–17
plants in teams 109
players, networks of 79

PowerPoint 20
practice codes of 91
   see also IfL code of professional
     practice
preparation for lessons 19–21
Preparing to Teach in the Lifelong
   Learning Sector (PTLLS) 96–7
Professional Graduate Certificate in
   Education (PGCE) 98–9
professional integrity, as a principle of the
   IfL code of professional practice 93
professional knowledge 91
professional practice, as a principle of the
   IfL code of professional practice 93
professional qualifications to teach *see*
   teaching qualifications
professional standards, Lifelong Learning
   UK (LLUK) 92
Professional Standards for QTLS
   assessment 49
   concepts of quality 1
   culture, ethos and values 75
   external inspection 28
   internal inspection 39
   listening to learners and evaluating
     learners' experience 61
   professionalism and accountability 90
   QA and QI 115
   quality in the classroom 14
   teamwork 104
professional values 91
professionalism 22–3, 92–6, 99–100
   accountability and 22, 90–1
   case studies 101–2
   defining 91
   organisational effectiveness and
     personal 122–4
   case study 122–3
   top tips 96
'provider performance review' process 42
PTLLS (Preparing to Teach in the Lifelong
   Learning Sector) 96–7
Putting Quality into Practice 7

QA
   defining 4
   focus 10–12
   introduction within post-compulsory
     education 7–10
   case studies 7–8

QA in assessment 53–6
teacher involvement 56–7
case study 56–7
QA system 28–9
meaning for providers 29
QAA (The Quality Assurance Agency for
Higher Education) 36
QI
defining 5
and participant feedback 61
QI of assessment
teacher involvement 56–7
case study 56–7
QTLS, Professional Standards *see*
Professional Standards for QTLS
qualifications, teaching *see* teaching
qualifications
quality
collaborative nature 121–4
concepts *see* concepts of quality
defining 2–3
link with funding 9, 42, 56, 87, 112–13
case study 112–13
as marketing 117
see also total quality
quality assurance *see* QA
Quality Assurance Agency for Higher
Education (QAA) 36
*The Quality Assurance System for Post-16
Education and Training Provision* 28
quality in the classroom 14–26
quality gurus 6–7
quality improvement *see* QI
quality industry 62
'Quality is Free' 6
quality lessons 15–26
case studies 24–6
delivering 94
Ofsted grading standards criteria 19,
21, 22, 23, 24
personalisation 21–2
planning *see* planning for learning
preparation 19–21
and professionalism 22–3
proving it 23–4
quality management
development as a policy and a process
5–6
models 3
see also Total Quality Management

(TQM)
quality reviews 40
quality trilogy 6
questioning techniques 17, 23

Raising Skills, Improving Life Chances 92
'Reactionnaires' 67
reasonable care, as a principle of the IfL
code of professional practice 93
record keeping 9
maintaining accurate 95
see also paper work and form-filling;
registers
'reflective discussions' 43
registers 7–8
case studies of use 7–8
resource investigators in teams 109
resources
and inclusive practice 87
for lessons 19–20, 94
respect
as a principle of the IfL code of
professional practice 93
responsibility 91
individual versus collective 105
to the IfL 93
retention, as a measure of outcomes 57
rituals and college/organisation culture 79

safeguarding young people and
vulnerable adults 95, 100–1
case study 101
SATs 51
Self Assessment Reports (SARs) 33
self-assessment 45–6
self-regulation 46–8
case study 47–8
shapers in teams 108
shared vision 77
Shrewsbury College, case study of
Advanced Practitioners (APs) 25–6
Single Voice for Self Regulation 46
social norms 106
specialists in teams 109
sponsoring bodies 29
staff
evaluation of 41
see also teachers
stakeholder voice
and the Framework for Excellence (FfE)

62–4

see also learner voice

standards

Lifelong Learning UK (LLUK) 92

maintenance of 62

QTLS *see* Professional Standards for QTLS

stories and college/organisation culture 79

Stories From the Front Line: the Impact of Inspection on Practitioners 32

Student Consultative groups 70–1

student evaluation

first point of contact 65–6

implementation 71–2

ownership of outcomes 71–3

philosophy 66–7

tools 67–71

course programme evaluation 68, 70–1

subject/module evaluation 67–8, 69f

student voice *see* learner voice

sub-cultures within the college/ organisation culture 79–80

case study 80

subject knowledge, enhancing 119-20

subject-specific organisations 120t

subject/module evaluation by students 67–8, 69f

success

celebrating 82

relationship between funding and 112–13

case study 112–13

success rates 57–8, 111

benchmarking using 58–9

as a measure of outcomes 58

summative assessment 17, 23

teachers

appropriate dress and behaviour 94–5

creative 19–20

effect of attitudes on college culture 76

involvement in the QA and QI

elements of assessment 56–7

case study 56–7

outstanding 14

reaction to assessment 51

see also associate teachers

teaching

actions to take to QA 119–21

enhance subject knowledge 119–20

improve knowledge of assessment strategies and skills in making assessment decisions 120

keeping up to date 121

know and understand the data 119

use of critical appraisal 121

observation of *see* observation

see also 'full teaching role'; inclusive teaching

Teaching & Learning Coaches (TLCs), case study 101–2

teaching qualifications 96–100

A1 – Vocational Assessor Award 99

Certificate in Education/Certificate in Higher Education (Cert Ed/Cert HE) 98

Certificate in Teaching in the Lifelong Learning Sector (CTLLS) 97

Diploma in Teaching in the Lifelong Learning Sector (DTLLS) 97–8

Preparing to Teach in the Lifelong Learning Sector (PTLLS) 96–7

Professional Graduate Certificate in Education (PGCE) 98–9

V1 – Vocational Internal Verifiers Award 99

team roles *see* Belbin's team roles model

team workers 109

teamwork 104–14

effective *see* effective teamwork

ineffective 111

organisational culture and 105–7

case study 105

testing 125

TLCs (Teaching & Learning Coaches), case study 101–2

Tomlinson Report (2004) 50

total quality, definition 6

Total Quality Control 6

Total Quality Management (TQM) 6, 7, 124

Toyota 117

trades unions 121

Tuckman's lifecycle of groups 110–11

forming 110

norming 111

performing 111

storming 110–11

tutorial support for learners 86

V1 – Vocational Internal Verifiers Award
   99–100
'Value Added' (VA) 59, 72
values
   professional 91
   shared 78–9
   sharing 81
   verification 54–5
vocational awards, verification for 54, 55
vulnerable adults
   defining 100

safeguarding *see* safeguarding young
   people and vulnerable adults

We Can Work it Out 20
widening participation, defining 83
working in teams *see* teamwork

young people, safeguarding *see*
   safeguarding young people and
   vulnerable adults

Zero Defects, concept 6